JEWISH SITES OF ISTANBUL
A GUIDE BOOK

ILAN KARMI

THE ISIS PRESS
ISTANBUL

First Edition

Published by
The Isis Press,
Şemsibey Sokak 10,
Beylerbeyi 81210 Istanbul
Tel: 321 38 51

ISBN 975-428-035-5

Printed in Turkey

CONTENTS

This guidebook has been the outcome of a persistent and combined endeavour put forward by a group of people dedicated to the study of Turkish Judaism. Having a firm determination to expose the charm of this one-time glorious — yet somewhat forgotten — community, an exciting journey into the past has been launched.

An impressive mosaic composed of ancient monuments such as decayed synagogues, medieval gravestones, well-ornamented private houses and well-known learning institutions, has been revealed in the course of this fascinating journey.

But first and foremost, this guide is the story of the members of the Istanbul Jewish community who in the course of nearly a millenium managed to maintain a flourishing community. Even today, the impact of the relatively small local Jewish community over the city's cultural and economic life is remarkable.

Many forces have joined together to make this guide possible: community leaders, members of the local Jewish clubs, scholars and journalists, the staff of several libraries and archives, colleagues and friends — to whom I am deeply indebted. Special thanks are reserved to both Ann Brener and Michael Lechuna who carefully reviewed the manuscript.

Hopefully, this guide will motivate visitors from all over the world to visit Istanbul and its historical monuments — Jewish and non-Jewish alike. Thus, the heritage of the Jewish community of Istanbul will be preserved and properly appreciated.

ISTANBUL AS A COSMOPOLITAN CITY

Once the capital of a sprawling empire composed of a mosaic-like ethnic populace, Istanbul emerged as one of the most diverse and cosmopolitan cities in the world. People of varied backgrounds, both religious and cultural, have long resided side by side in the various quarters of the city. Each major neighborhood of Istanbul blends a vast array of ethno-religious heritages. Streets, courtyards and even apartment buildings often boast residents of the most diverse origin.

Consequently, a visitor to districts such as Galata and Kuzguncuk will find synagogues, churches and mosques nestling side by side. Religious festivities tend to highlight this unique harmony. The respect and affection of the neighborhood residents for each other results in mutual participation in various religious and social functions, which an outsider can only view with wonder and surprise. The Christmas celebrations, for instance, draw a throng of local visitors both Muslim and Jewish to the city's various Catholic churches.

Ever since the Ottoman conquest of Istanbul, non-Muslims have played an important role in the economic, social, cultural and political life of the city. In some cases, a certain occupation was traditionally shared by the members of a specific group; in other cases, members of different groups worked together in the same field. While peaceful relations generally prevailed amongst the various non-Muslim congregations, conflicts were not unknown. Strife due to economic competition often flared up, and only government intervention restored equanimity and smoothed ruffled feelings.

The modernization of Istanbul can be fully

appreciated only by taking into consideration the role of the local non-Muslims. Their access to Western civilization and commerce rendered them a natural link between East and West. Western schools, (such as the American Robert College, today's Bosphoros University) which sprung up during the 19th century have remained a model of excellence to this very day.

The many foreigners who made Istanbul into their headquarters have contributed to the cosmopolitan and colorful character of the city. Galata (today's Beyoğlu), inhabited for centuries by both foreigners and local non-Muslims, emerged as an animated quarter as modern as any that the Western world had to offer. One such example is İstiklal Caddesi, the neighborhood's main thoroughfare, a mirror of the architectural trends and fancies that swept through the capitals of Europe.

The many non-Muslims who once swarmed through the streets of Istanbul, particularly in Galata, have now dwindled to the tiniest of minorities. Of these minorities the Armenians, the Jews and the Greek-Orthodox compose the largest groups. Both the Catholic and the Assyrian Churches, in addition to other smaller congregations, maintain age-old rituals in the city.

Yet, infinitesimal though they are in numbers (less than 1% of the total population), their impact resounds in the commercial and cultural life of the city. Indeed their influence even surpasses boundaries, and the locally elected Greek-Orthodox patriarch rules over a congregation dispersed over several countries.

Newspapers in both Turkish and ethnic languages contribute to the vibrant life of these minority groups. There are two Armenian daily newspapers, *Jamanak* and *Marmara*; two Greek dailies, *Apovyematini* and *Iho*; plus a Jewish weekly *Şalom*, and the Armenian periodicals *Kulis* and *Sirp Burgic*. Issues mailed abroad included, the total circulation of these publications never exceeds ten thousand.

Yet the color and charm added by the small

ethnic groups has not completely faded. A continuous flow of immigrants from both the provinces and neighboring countries fills the city with blond blue-eyed Bulgarians, stately black-haired natives from the Black Sea region, and slant-eyed Uzbeks from Central Asia.

Significant though the role of the Jewish community has been in all aspects of city life, its importance was not limited to Istanbul. Ottoman-Jewish history in particular, and indeed World Jewish history in general, have witnessed the tremendous impact of this diligent community.

A substantial Jewish community has prospered in Istanbul (known in Jewish sources as Kushta or Kostadina) ever since the tumultuous days of 1453. In that year, the Ottoman Turks conquered the Byzantine city of Constantinople that had been for over a millenium the capital of the Eastern Roman Empire.

This already thriving Jewish community was considerably reinforced by the Jewish refugees fleeing post-expulsion Spain in 1492. The Ottoman Sultan Beyazit II, more than pleased to welcome these skilled and resourceful fugitives, could only express astonishment that the Catholic monarchs of Spain should thus enrich his country to the detriment of their own.

Located in the very administrative core of the Ottoman state, the influence of Istanbul's Jewish community exceeded its geographical boundaries. Prompted by the government's policy of centralization, the capital's Jewish leadership accumulated wide authority over the provincial Jewish communities, mainly in the early and late Ottoman periods. Istanbul set the mold and fashion for all aspects of community life throughout the Ottoman realm.

Spiritual inspiration and material support streamed from the Istanbul Jewish community to the many and far-flung Jewish communities in the eastern Mediterranean basin. Even though not many

Jews left Istanbul for Palestine prior to 1948, Istanbul Jews played a crucial role in the creation of the Zionist movement. Their intervention was essential for the momentous meeting that took place between **Theodore Herzel**, the Father of Zionism, and Abdülhamid II, the reigning Ottoman sultan in the 1890's.

As in times of peace, so also in times of emergency. Thus many Jewish refugees who escaped the Russian pogroms in the 19th century managed to start life afresh in the warm and welcoming atmosphere of Istanbul. And under the shadow of World War II, a not insignificant number of German-Jewish scholars found refuge in Istanbul, where their professional eminence was greatly appreciated by Turkish academic institutions.

Thanks to the neutrality proclaimed by the Turkish government on the eve of World War II, Istanbul Jews escaped the bitter destiny of their co-religionists in German-occupied Europe. Turkish Jewry was once again swept up in the currents of World history. Once more they played a crucial role in the feverish diplomatic efforts for the salvation of European Jewry. Neither did they fail to offer every possible assistance to the Jewish refugees who managed to cross over the border to find a safe haven in Turkey.

* * *

Already in Roman times Jews lived in the city later to be known as Istanbul. In 1176, the famous Jewish traveller, **Benjamin de Tudela**, found nearly 2,555 Jews there. Some of these Jews, the Romaniots, had lived there for centuries; others had come from Italy as merchants. Due to persistent persecution under Byzantine rule which included forced conversion and expulsion, the number of Jews gradually declined. Those who remained in the city were confined to a special district (Pera: today's Beyoğlu).

Though some Jews were inevitably harmed by the

vicissitudes of war, an alleged agreement between the Jews and the Ottoman conqueror, Sultan Mehmed II, prior to the 1453 conquest of the city, enabled them to smoothly adapt themselves to the new rule.

Coming from far and wide, from both within and without the Ottoman territories a massive influx of Jews settled in the city, the new capital of the expanding Ottoman Empire. Government officials looked favorably on such developments, which brought prosperity and repopulated the war-depleted lands.

Consequently, the local Jewish community of Istanbul expanded enormously in the subsequent years. The 1492 and 1497 expulsions of Jews from Spain and Portugal were followed by the largest and most significant wave of Jewish immigration to Ottoman Istanbul.

Napkin in the Istanbul tradition with "Zion and two Commandments"

In the 16th century, Istanbul constituted the second largest Jewish community in the Ottoman Empire. Only Saloniki could boast a larger community. Jews who were involved in various fields of activity, left a remarkable impact on many facets of city life. Their contribution was significantly enhanced by Jews from the Iberian Peninsula who transferred their skills, experience and rich cultural heritage to their new homeland.

Several prominent Jews reached high-level positions in the Ottoman court and central administration, as advisors to the Sultan, court physicians, local governors and diplomats. Amongst them, one should mention in particular **Moses Hamon**, chief physician to Sultan Süleyman the Magnificent, the physician **Solomon Askenazi** who brought about the surrender of the city of Buda to the Ottomans, and the legendary **Ester Kiera** who served as an intermediary for the women of the Imperial Harem in their contacts with the outside world. The most influential Jew was, however, the Lisbon-born **Don Joseph Nasi** (1514-1579). Don Joseph and his well-known aunt **Dona Gracia Mendes**, were celebrated for their large-scale philantropic endeavors which included the founding of educational institutions and the attempted rebuilding of the Galilean city of Tiberias as a Jewish center. In return for his services to the Ottoman throne, Don Joseph was rewarded with the title of "Duke of Naxos".

But this first flowering could not last forever. A process of decline set in during the course of the 17th and 18th centuries for various reasons: natural disasters as well as increasing competition from local Greek financiers and merchants. Internal strife over questions of political power only intensified the growing instability of the community. Government intervention to restore the status quo was not an infrequent occurence.

This transitional period brought about profound demographic changes as well. Natural disasters such as fires and earthquakes were not without their silver lining, as many Jewish residents took the opportunity to move into the more modernized districts of the city.

Thus, in the 19th century, Galata evolved as the unchallenged modern quarter of the capital when the older neighborhoods of Hasköy and Balat waned into insignificance. The Jewish residents who flocked to Galata in increasing numbers brought about the transfer of leading communal institutions to this quarter. European Jews fleeing persecution greatly contributed to the modernization process of Istanbul. Thus, for example, a group of Russian Jewish tailors who found shelter in Galata utilized their Western training to promote the local garnment industry.

In the 19th century, nearly 40 active synagogues provided the focus for the more than 60,000 Jews residing in Istanbul. Whereas the material conditions of most Jews left them huddled in the older neighborhoods, the more fortunate ones who moved to the affluent districts of the city often found their way to the upper echelons of the local elite.

In the late 19th and early 20th centuries, the Jews of Istanbul witnessed a period of cultural and economic revival thanks to the comprehensive reforms initiated by the Ottoman policy-makers. These reforms, known in Turkish history as *Tanzimat*, had a profound impact on the legal, social and economic status of the Jews.

Under the new laws that granted non-Muslims legal equality, Jews succeeded in transforming the very fabric of their life, largely through the modern educational system. Graduates of prestigious schools, such as that of the Alliance Israélite Universelle, often assumed high positions not only within the Jewish environment, but also in the greater civil community as well.

Jews played an active role in the emerging pluralistic Ottoman society. Jewish delegates represented their co-religionists in the newly-established assemblies, such as the Beyoğlu Municipality (1857) and the first National Assembly in 1877.

The Ortaköy-born **Abraham Camondo** (1785-1873) was the major force behind the modernization of contemporary Istanbul Jewry. A politician, financier and philanthropist, Camondo extended great efforts on behalf of his co-religionists. Among other duties, he served as the regional president of the Alliance Israélite Universelle, as well as being a representative to the Beyoğlu Municipality and the founder of the well-known Camondo Institute.

Hebrew Pentateuch printed in Istanbul in 1505

Abraham Camondo symbolizes the modernist trends that sought to reform all spheres of educational and social life. No less symbolic was his final and tragic demise. Forced by reactionary circles within the Jewish community to retreat from dreams of reformation and growth, he was compelled to abandon Istanbul and died an exile's death in Paris. The almost regal cortège and façade of Jewish solidarity that accompanied his funeral bier could not compensate for the bitterness and rivalry that was the increasing lot of contemporary Ottoman Jewry.

The turbulent years prior to the collapse of the Ottoman Empire witnessed the dramatic events of the 1908 Young Turk Revolution. The Young Turks — who were at first enthusiastically supported by many Jews, particularly those of Saloniki (the birthplace of the movement)— sought to replace the dictatorship of **Sultan Abdülhamid II** with a more progressive regime. Though Jews as an ethnic minority were fairly treated by the deposed Sultan, as the synagogue named after the deposed monarch testifies (the **Hemdat Israel synagogue** in the neighborhood of Haydarpaşa), as citizens of a despotic system they could not but welcome the promised reforms.

But disappointment was not slow to set in as one political expectation after another proved an illusion.

Indeed, several Jews were amongst the first delegates of the 1908 Parliament, and an affirmation of civil rights for all was guaranteed. Yet as the guiding principles of justice and equality gradually receded in importance, the Jews found themselves in a disadvantageous position no less than other sectors of the population. Such were the events that brought about the increasing Jewish emigration to other countries, especially in North and South America.

World War I put an end not only to the Ottoman State but also to the unique position of Istanbul Jewry as a leading community in a far-flung Empire. The floundering of the old system, even as the revolutionary reforms of the new one were being fostered, threw the Turkish Jewish community into a state of confusion and doubt. Their terms of reference had altered; no longer protected by imperial firmans and guarantees of autonomy, the religious minorities of the new Republic were guaranteed civil rights by the Lausanne Accords.

However, the Jewish citizens of the Turkish Republic soon opted to cut loose from the old system and placed themselves firmly within the new framework of Republican society. The democratic-secular orientation of the new regime offered Turkish Jews more security than the somewhat vague guarantees of the Western powers.

In the course of the following years, the Jews of Istanbul underwent two subsequent demographic changes that reflected the events of the times: (1) though no longer the capital, Istanbul maintained its pre-eminence as many Jews left the provinces to reside there; (2) nonetheless, a population drain came about when many Jews left Istanbul to settle in the newly-formed State of Israel in the post-1948 era.

Jewish emigration on a lesser scale resulted from various political upheavals during the following decades, such as the 1955 anti-minority riots (directed chiefly against local Greeks) and the period of anarchy preceeding the military intervention of 1980.

Revolutions and emigrations notwithstanding, there remains in Istanbul a flourishing congregation of some 18,000 Jews. Most of them belong to the middle and upper classes and reside in the more affluent districts of the city. Braced by even-handed government policy and enjoying good relations with their non-Jewish fellow citizens, the Jews of Istanbul are well-integrated in all aspects of this vibrant city. It is for this reason that the terrorist act of September 6, 1986, which left 21 worshippers in the Neve Şalom Synagogue dead, so abruptly and unexpectedly shattered the wonted peace of the city. On this devastating occasion Turkish citizens representing the entire spectrum of political views and religious orientation, joined ranks to condemn this brutal attack perpetrated by outside terrorists.

The Jews of this great city make every effort to preserve their glorious heritage. The Chief Rabbinate and the Community Councils have been instrumental in this endeavour. Worshippers throng the various synagogues of the city in order to celebrate the Jewish holidays throughout the year. And it is not holidays alone that witness such activity; some 10 synagogues hold daily services.

Well-equipped social clubs provide for the cultural needs of the community. The youth have their cultural and sport clubs (such as *Amikal* which was established in 1910), while those of the older generation find a wide variety of programs more suited to their own interests. Neither have music and theater been neglected. Enterprising members of the young generation have formed a musical group, **Los Paşaros Sefardim** (The Spanish Birds), dedicated to the revival of traditional Jewish-Spanish music. Several members of the Jewish community achieved prominent status in the country's cultural and intellectual life. To mention only a few: the journalist **Sami Kohen**, the conductor **Yeşua Aroya**, the writer **Mario Levi** and the actress **Rozet Hubeş**.

The weekly Jewish newspaper Şalom and the bulletins published by the Jewish clubs record the major events of the community. The warmth of the summer season finds a substantial number of Jews in their vacation homes on the Princes' Islands, where life revolves around the local synagogues and clubs.

The Jews of Istanbul preserve regular contacts with other Jewish communities in the country. The second largest Jewish community of Turkey, that of İzmir, is relatively independent and maintains various cultural activities of its own. A dwindling population has been the fate of some of the smaller Jewish communities, such as Bursa and Edirne, where communal activities have nearly ceased. Thus, the Jewish community of Istanbul is now recognized as the political, financial and economic center of Turkish Jewry.

1992 ushers in the 500th anniversary of the arrival of the Spanish Jews in Turkey. Warmly encouraged by the Turkish authorities, the local community has initiated a large-scale project to renovate and preserve the remains of a magnificent heritage. This endeavour has re-established the formerly languishing ties between the Istanbul community and the Turkish-Jewish diaspora, resettled mainly in Israel and the United States.

Once again Istanbul has resumed its traditional role of eminence for Turkish Jewry.

LOS PAŞAROS
SEFARADİS

JEWISH COMMUNAL INSTITUTIONS

The Chief Rabbinate

The supreme representative body of Turkish Jewry is the chief rabbinate. The origins of this institution date back to the early Ottoman period. According to local tradition, the first chief rabbi, **Moses Capsali** (d. 1499), was appointed by the Ottoman Sultan, Mehmed the Conqueror, soon after the 1453 conquest of the city. This chief rabbi was granted wide jurisdiction over his co-religionists in the Ottoman realm, similar to the status granted to the Greek-Orthodox and Armenian patriarchs.

The dominant status of the chief rabbinate was gradually eroded following the demise of the second chief rabbi, **Elija Mizrahi** (d. 1526). As a result of this development, community members took upon themselves an increasingly active role in all aspects of congregational administration. Rabbinic authority became confined to strictly spiritual issues.

Yet rabbinical circles were not left entirely powerless. Ottoman authority had vested in them means such as excommunication that enabled the rabbis to preserve an active presence in communal affairs.

An ever continuing process of change and modification characterized the institution of the chief rabbinate throughout the 19th and early 20th centuries. The rabbis were confronted with strong opposition from the emerging secular forces advocating modernization and liberalization. The chief rabbi's status and power were re-defined in contemporary regulations issued by the Government upon Jewish request.

Powerful as the first chief rabbi had been, it was

only under the tenure of the influential **Haim Nahum** (1908-1920) that the title "chief rabbi" was officially given to the incumbent.

The disintegration of the Ottoman Empire could not but diminish the chief rabbinate's authority as the Jewish population was steadily drained to other centers. Further decline in the status of this institution followed the post World War I formation of the secular Republic of Turkey. Following the demise of Chief Rabbi **Moshe Becerano** in 1931, the Jewish community was left with no elected chief rabbi for nearly 20 years. Despite several obstacles, the chief rabbinate was after wards officially recognized by the Turkish government. Respected and honored by the Turkish authorities, the chief rabbis frequently conduct ceremonial meetings with Government officials and visiting State dignitaries.

The present chief rabbi, **David Asseo**, was elected in 1961. Born in Istanbul in 1914, he was educated in the local Alliance Israélite Universelle school and in the Rabbinical Seminary of Rhodes. Having served as both teacher and rabbi of the local Italian congregation, Asseo officiated as a member of the Jewish court (*Beit-Din*), as the director of the Hasköy-based Rabbinical Seminary, and as assistant to the former chief rabbi, Raphael Saban, prior to being himself elected chief rabbi. Rabbi Asseo ranks as the 32nd chief rabbi since since the appointment of Capsali in 1453. Highly-educated and knowledgeable in both local and international affairs, Rabbi Asseo is the esteemed and honored leader of the community.

The chief rabbi is assisted by a *Beit-Din* composed of four rabbis. Local chief rabbis outside of Istanbul are subordinate to the latter. A dignified and time-mellowed building serves as the headquarters for the chief rabbinate. Extensive activities concerning all aspects of religious life are carried out from this center. Prior to the formation of the central chief rabbinate in the early 20th century, each Jewish neighborhood maintained a separate rabbinate and court.

The chief rabbinate is represented by local rabbis

and *gabbais* (officers of a synagogue) throughout the Jewish neighborhoods of the city. Together they conduct the religious services that consecrate weddings, *Bar-Mitzvas*, and funerals. The presence of leading figures adds lustre to important communal events. Such an occasion is the annual service held to commemorate the victims of the Neve Şalom massacre in 1986. In accordance with the timeless Jewish tradition followed by well-established communities, Istanbul assists remote Jewish communities well beyond its geographical boundaries in matters both spiritual and cultural.

Although *kosher* restaurants no longer exist in Istanbul, — though the newly opened five-star Swisshotel's restaurant offers *Kosher* meals — there is nevertheless a ready supply of ritually-butchered meat and special Passover *Matzot* (unleavened bread) produced in the *Matzot* factory operated by the community within the Galata neighborhood.

Chief Rabbinate: 23 Yemenici Sokak, Beyoğlu/Tünel, Tel: 2448794/95

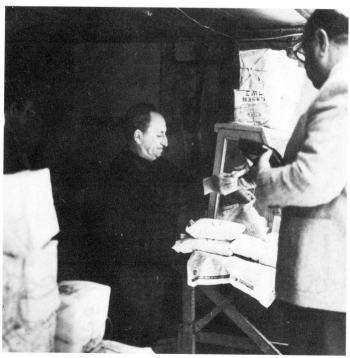

Balıkçı Abraham: Kosher Fishseller in Galata

Community Council

Along with the chief rabbinate there is also a council (*Konsey Laik*) selected by the chief rabbi once every 3 years. The council's president is co-opted from among the 21 members of the council on an annual basis. Assisting the chief rabbi, the council meets in the building of the chief rabbinate. Members of this council represent the non-religious elements of the community. Entrusted with matters of education and culture, the council's members administer various social institutions such as schools and clubs.

The peaceful coexistence reigning between these two representative bodies is an expression of a compromise achieved only after decades of bitter struggle for power. This present balance is in fact the result of decades of conflicts between waring factions at the turn of the century.

In addition to the aforementioned institutions, each neighborhood has a local council composed of elected officials. The activities of such councils generally revolve around the neighborhood synagogue. Ten such local councils located in the synagogues, function in Jewish-inhabited neighborhoods of Istanbul.

The Ashkenazi and Italian congregations of Istanbul maintain separate, government-sanctioned councils. Unlike the Karaite congregation, these councils are subordinate to the central rabbinical institutions.

Office of the Ashkenazi congregation: 10 Banker Sokak, Karaköy (Tel: 2442975)
Office of the Italian congregation: 17/1, Küçük Hendek Sokak, Karaköy (Tel: 2447784)

Synagogues

At least 40 synagogues served the Jewish community of Istanbul during its heyday. Since synagogues commanded allegiance not only according to neighborhood but even according to geographical origin of the worshippers, it is not uncommon to find several synagogues side by side.

So fine and varied were the considerations that prompted community loyalty that synagogue congregations were even further delineated according to social status. Thus, for instance, the Ashkenazim of the city established two separate synagogues in the late 19th century: one for the elite and one for the lower classes. Often, we find synagogues lined up one after the other according to the geographical location of the members' cities of origin, as though to construct of wood and stone a veritable map of the Diaspora. One such example are the four synagogues of the Balat neighborhood (Saloniki, Ahrida, Castoria and Ichtipol) named all of them after cities in Macedonia.

Many and varied were the tasks of the synagogues. Serving not only as the house of worship, they also functioned as local community centers and meeting places. To a large extent, the history of the synagogue is the history of the community. When messianic fervor swept through the Jewish world in the mid-17th century, it was in the synagogue of Balat that the local Jews first came into direct contact with the self-proclaimed Messiah **Sabbatai Zevi**. And in the mid-19th century, it was in the Shalom synagogue of Galata that the community leadership, under the auspices of **Sir Moses Montifiore**, issued their call for the promotion of the Turkish language amongst Ladino-speaking Jews.

Few are the neighborhoods in Istanbul that lack synagogues. Some (such as Haydarpaşa) contain only one; others (such as Galata) contain as many as five. The oldest one is the Ahrida Synagogue in the neighborhood of Balat dating back to the Byzantine period. This synagogue, like most others, has undergone a continuous series of restorations. Destructions wrought by fires and earthquakes, as well as the decay of time, have left their mark on most synagogues of the city. Others were simply abandoned as their worshippers moved to new neighborhoods

Recently, the local community has undertaken measures to preserve some of its oldest and more picturesque synagogues. Most active synagogues conduct daily services — although the number of participants is not great. Others are open only on certain holidays, such as Yanbol synagogue which opens its doors only on the holiday of Succot. Major occasions find the community and its leaders assembled in one of the largest synagogues. Tradition is strong, and certain services are carried out only in one particular synagogue that has been hallowed for this specific ritual.

Many of the oldest synagogues of the city are perilously close to disintegration and are accordingly closed to the public (such as Ichtipol synagogue in Balat). And in certain places only the mere remains of a gate or wall indicate the presence of some ancient synagogues (as in the case of the Saloniki synagogue of Balat).

List of active synagogues

Neve Şalom (61 Büyük Hendek Sokak, Şişhane, tel: 2441576)
Ashkenazi (37 Yüksek Kaldırım Sokak, Karaköy, tel: 2442975)
Italian (27 Şair Ziya Paşa Sokak, Karaköy, tel: 2447784)
Beth Israel (4 Efe Sokak, Osmanbey, tel: 1406599)
Hemdat Israel (35 İzzetin Sokak, Haydarpaşa, tel: 3365293)
Göztepe/Caddebostan (8 Taş Mektep Sokak, Göztepe, tel: 3565922)
Etz-Ahayim (40/1 Muallim Naci Caddesi, Ortaköy, tel: 2601896)
Beth Ya'akov (8 İcadiye Caddesi, Kuzguncuk, tel: 3431699 - summer)
Virano (8 Yakup Sokak, Kuzguncuk-winter)
Ahrida (51 Kürkçü Çesme Sokak, Balat, tel: 2234729)
Yanbol (1 Ayan Sokak, Balat; open only on Succot)
Sirkeci (1 İstasyon Arkası Sokak, Sirkeci, tel: 5133043)
Bakırköy (Cumhuriyet Sokak, Zeytinlik Mahallesi, Bakırköy, tel: 5425102)
Yeniköy (242 Köybaşı Sokak, Yeniköy, tel: 2513781)
Bnai-Mikra Karaite (3 Mahlul Sokak, Hasköy)
Hesed Leavraam, Büyükada (5 Pancur Sokak, Büyükada, tel:3823788)
Burgazada (2 Köy Kahyası Sokak, Burgazada, tel: 3518549)
Beth-Ya'akov, (12 Orhan Sokak, Heybeliada)

Wedding ceremony at Neve Shalom synagogue

Communal Institutions

(1) HOSPITAL: The community maintains one hospital, Or-Ahayim, housed in a handsome building erected in 1899. Located in the district of Balat, the hospital at present serves a largely non-Jewish local population. (For further information see "Balat").
Or-Ahayim Hospital : 162 Debbek Sokak, Balat, Tel: 5241156/2457841/

(2) OLD-AGE HOME: Nearly 100 senior members of the Jewish community reside in an impressive home in the neighborhood of Hasköy, a building formerly belonging to the Alliance Israélite Universelle.
Old Age Home (İhtiyarlara Yardım Derneği/Moşav Zekinim): Hasköy (Tel: 2536084 / 2506988)

(3) PHILANTHROPIC SOCIETIES: Long noted for its well-organized communal work, the Istanbul Jewish community of the early 20th century featured a network of nearly a dozen such benevolent organizations. Wealthy and enlightened members of the community invested great efforts in these organizations that fostered a more cohesive social texture among their Jewish brethern. Such was the Society of Jewish Women of Pera and Galata, founded in 1893, to assist the poor and widowed of the community.

Currently, the community maintains several charity organizations, such as: *Matan Beseter Bikur Holim* (tel: 2497937); *Sadaka Umarpe* (2446022); *Mişne Tora* supporting poor students (tel: 2449190). Most organizations are attached to the Chief Rabbinate and the central synagogues.

(4) SCHOOLS: The Jewish community formerly run a well-developed school system for both secular and religious needs. Prior to the 19th century the community-sponsored *Yeshivot* (Religious Schools) offered the only public education available. Wealthy Jewish dignitaries, such as Don Joseph Nasi, vied with the chief rabbinate for the honor of supporting such schools.

Winds of change in the 19th century brought about significant reforms in the educational system. Foreign organizations, the French-based Alliance Israélite Universelle (AIU), in particular, along with local Jewish magnates (such as Abraham Camondo) combined efforts to introduce modern westernized education. Such was the impact of reform that modern education was now made available to girls.

These reforms were not without their political aspects. Indeed, the struggle between religious and secular education was in fact a harbinger of greater political and social issues, which would determine the very fabric of an increasingly modernized society.

Neither were educational possibilities narrowed to the choice between religious and secular schools: Individual congregations, eager to foster community values and needs, also supported schools of their own (such as the Ashkenazi school of Galata); vocational schools offered their students the chance to acquire modern professional skills.

Jewish children were not necessarily limited to their own communal schools. State schools established in the second half of the 19th century offered additional possibilities. Indeed, Jewish graduates of schools such as the reputed Galatasaray Lycée, often reached the higher echelons of Turkish public life. Missionary schools, with an ever-open eye to conversion, were also eager to attract Jewish pupils. Though parents were not unaware of the inherent dangers, they nevertheless often succumbed to the cosmopolitan atmosphere of these schools, and the lure of free tuition. In view of all these options, it is not surprising that countless Jewish families found themselves torn between traditional religious values and the unfamiliar demands of a burgeoning westernized society. The *Kosher* food made available to Jewish pupils of modern State schools by order of the Sultan himself helped to ease somewhat the pangs of conscience of many a bewildered parent. The very language of instruction was in itself a point of contention. A curriculum taught in German in one school might be taught in French or English in another. The Hebrew and Turkish languages had claims of their own as well.

Jewish children in Istanbul of the 1990's find themselves with three educational options. The choice of schools is by and large determined by socio-economic considerations. Only two Jewish schools, one elementary and a high school, still offer a traditional-religious education. Located in Galata, these schools are operated by the Jewish community, even though a majority of the school staff is no longer Jewish. Of the many buildings that once housed Jewish educational institutions, a number have been abandoned while others now serve new functions of the community.

Jewish Primary School (Musevi Karma İlkokulu), Şişhane, tel: 2443170
Jewish High School (Beyoğlu Özel Musevi Lisesi, Şişhane), tel: 2555237

Yet by far the greater portion of Jewish children attend State public schools. The Şişli-Teşvikiye neighborhood schools, considered among the best secular schools in Turkey, have a high enrollment of Jewish pupils. The ranks of the Jewish upper-middle class are largely composed of graduates of these schools.

Wealthier families tend to enroll their children in private schools noted for their European ambience in addition to their academic excellence. The former missionary schools continue to be in great demand, especially since conversionary efforts constitute no longer any lurking danger. The German school of Beyoğlu, founded by Protestant missionaries in the 19th century, is particularly favored.

The Bosphoros University of Istanbul (formery the American Robert College) attracts many Jewish students. Istanbul University and Marmara University, though less fashionable, also have a high enrollment of Jewish students as has the Istanbul Technical University.

Jewish children, even those enrolled in secular schools, almost invariably attend Sunday school courses and programs in Jewish education under the guidance of the *Mahzike Tora* Society (Tel: 2406599). Cultural enrichment programs on a wide variety of subjects, including Jewish history, are a popular activity in the Jewish youth clubs.

(5) JEWISH CULTURAL CENTERS AND CLUBS: Istanbul Jewry has long maintained a rich variety of clubs, both social and cultural. Four active clubs currently serve the needs of the Jewish population of both banks of the city: Şişli-Nişantaş (the European side) and Göztepe-Erenköy (the Asian side). The clubs, under the direction of elected officials, are the venue for holiday festivities and major events.
Jewish Club in Şişli (Dostluk Yurdu Derneği): Tel: 2483336
Jewish Club in Göztepe (Kültür Derneği): Tel: 3504192

The *Amikal* Youth Club, located in the neighborhood of Şişli and established in 1910, is still the vibrant meeting place of the young generation.

The local Jewish sports club provides an amicable meeting ground for budding young athletes.

Jewish Youth Club (Arkadaşlık Yurdu Derneği-Amikal) in Şişli: Tel: 2406599

Jewish Sports Club (Yıldırım) in Şişli: Tel: 2408370

The Jewish weekly newspaper *Şalom*, whose editorial offices are located in the district of Nişantaş, records the major events and cultural activities of the community.

Şalom Gazetesi, Gözlem Gazetecilik, Kuyulu Bostan Sokak, Mola Apt. 3/2, Nişantaş, 80200, Istanbul. Tel: 247 30 82/ 240-41-44. Editor: Mr. Silvio Ovadia.

The preparations for the 500th anniversary celebrating the arrival of Spanish Jewry in Turkey (1492-1992) are being coordinated by the 500th Year Foundation, Mecidiyeköy, Istanbul. (The Quincentennial Foundation, Cemal Sahir Sokak 26/78 Mecidiyeköy, tel: 2753944, fax: 2742607). The Committee's Secretary is Mr. Nedim Yahya.

Cemeteries

Jewish cemeteries are scattered all over the city. The oldest gravestones, dating back to the Byzantine period, were discovered in **Eğri Kapı,** near the walls of the old city. The newest cemeteries were erected in Ulus in the second half of the 20th century.

Istanbul's major Jewish cemeteries are located in the following neighborhoods: Hasköy (including a Karaite plot), Ortaköy, Şişli (Italian), Ulus (Ashkenazi and Sefardi), Haydarpaşa, Üsküdar (Dönme).

Jewish Sects and Congregations

The sectarian factor has played a predominant role in the life of the Jewish community of Istanbul ever since the early Ottoman period. The basic unit around which the individual's life revolved varied from period to period according to changing circumstances. Of the various considerations that governed the daily life of the ordinary individual, none was more important than the individual's place of origin.

The relations among the various Jewish congregations of the capital fluctuated from mutual collaboration to the most vehement disagreement. The number of congregations varied from period to period, each congregation often further divided into a hierarchy based on considerations such as class, occupation and cultural orientation. Ottoman archival sources indicate that as many as 40 origin-based congregations flourished in 17th-century Istanbul.

As a further demonstration of this point often the origin of a certain Jew in Istanbul could be traced by his family name. Indeed, members of various congregations share certain typical names. For instance, Chikoshwilly indicates a Georgian origin, and Alfandari an Arab one. Occasionally, due to certain considerations such as mixed marriages, it is difficult to trace a person's origin merely by his last name. Furthermore, some members of the community have now adopted Turkish names. Thus, Bahar became İpeker and Banunu Bana.

Congregations tended either to affiliate themselves with the rabbinate or to follow a non-rabbinate orientation (*i.e.* Orthodox - non Orthodox). The predominant rabbinate category was further subdivided into four groups:

A) *Romaniots:* The Romaniots were the Jewish inhabitants of Greece and Byzantium. Whereas some had been residents of Constantinople prior to the Ottoman conquest returning once the war was over, others were settled there by the new Ottoman masters intent on repopulating the capital. The Romaniots played an important role in the life of the city's Jewish community during the formative years of Ottoman rule. But with the passing of time, newcomers from abroad gradually usurped their position of influence, and the Romaniots ceased to exist as a separate congregation.

Nowadays, only an infinitesimal number of

Istanbul Jews can claim a direct relation to ancestors of Romaniot origin. Special customs and traditions often distinguished the Greek-speaking Romaniots from other local Jewish groups. Jews of Romaniot-Byzantine origin could be recognized by names such as Galimidi, Roditi and Galipapa.

The most visually impressive remnant of the Romaniot past is the Ahrida synagogue in the Balat district, which dates back to the distant Byzantine past. Remnants of tombstones carrying Byzantine names such as Abastasa were recently found near the walls of the old city.

B) Ashkenazim: Ashkenazi Jews of European origin had settled in Istanbul prior to the Ottoman conquest. The Ottoman victory ushered in a new era as Ashkenazi Jews swept in from the German lands, Austria, Hungary, Poland and Russia. Fleeing pogroms and antisemitism, these Jews found a welcoming haven, assisted and encouraged by the Ottoman government. The last massive wave of Ashkenazi immigration to Istanbul occurred in the late 19th and early 20th centuries, following the rise of nationalism and political upheaval. World War II found a wave of Ashkenazi Jews, and amongst them a number of eminent German professors, fleeing the Nazi menace.

In the early 20th century, the Ashkenazim constituted nearly 10% of the total Jewish population of Istanbul. Often retaining their original citizenships, they not infrequently enjoyed the support of Central European powers.

Ashkenazim flocked to the modern district of Galata, where they established a separate congregation according to the rituals of Ashkenaz. Only the Ashkenazi synagogue of Karaköy now remains (see "Galata"). Another synagogue formerly belonging to the Ashkenazi congregation was given to new-comers from Edirne in the early 20th century (see Edirneli synagogue in Galata). Sephardic rabbis have for the past 40 years presided over a congregation that numbers scarcely more than 1,000 Ashkenazis. The administration is handled by an elected committee subordinate to the central Jewish leadership. The Ashkenazi cemetery is located in the neighborhood of Ulus.

The most common Ashkenazi name is Ashkenazi or in its Turkish version Eskinazi; yet this family name exists among Jews of non-Ashkenazi origin as well. Jews of German origin bear names such as Rosenberg and Grünberg; Sarfati, Salians, etc., indicate a French origin.

C) *Italians:* Byzantine Constantinople had already contained a fair number of Jews hailing from Genoa, Venice and other cities of the Italian Peninsula. Another influx of Italian Jews, many of whom had taken refuge in Italy after fleeing the Spanish Inquisition, flocked to Istanbul following the Ottoman conquest.

Relations between Italian Jews and their co-religionists went through periods of growing tension. Already in 1555, the local Jews of Italian origin had attempted to form a separate congregation following a controversy over the boycott of the Italian city of Ancona. Unlike the rest of the community, Italian Jews opposed the punishment of Ancona for persecuting Jewish converts who fled there from Spain. The rift intensified in the 19th century, this time over the question of marriage. This case brought about the formation of a separate congregation headed by the Italian citizen **Daniel Paranadis**, with the support of other groups who rejected the Sephardic dominance, such as Jews of Greek and Bulgarian origin. Thus, the newly-formed congregation replaced the vanished Romaniot community.

The proud heritage of this congregation is reflected in the handsome synagogue of Karaköy (b. 1887) as well as the carefully tended cemetery of Şişli. Retaining Italian cizitenship to this very day, many of its members maintain close cultural and economic relations with Italy.

The Italian community of today administers its congregation of some 500 members through an elected council similar to that of the Ashkenazi Jews. The

Italian language and culture, once so predominant amongst Italian Jews, is today a fading and dwindling element in the life of the community.

Members of the Italian congregation can be identified by names such as Modiani ('Jew' in Italian), Mitrani, Romano, Pizante and Krespi.

D) Sephardim: The proclamation of **Sultan Bayazit II** in 1492 not only provided a safe refuge for exiled Spanish Jewry, but also wrought momentous changes for the city of Istanbul. So large was the first wave of Sephardic (*i.e.,* Spanish) immigrants that the Jewish population of the city more than doubled. The bearers of a magnificent cultural heritage, the Sephardim quickly established themselves as the leading social and economic force within local Jewry. The Spanish language of these émigrés was preserved in the Ladino (Judéo-Espagnol) spoken to this very day. That Ladino is spoken even today by so many local Jews is a measure of the impact made by Spanish Jewry.

Jewish shopkeepers

Thus, from the very outset of their arrival, the Sephardim formed the leading section of Istanbul Jewry, both culturally and numerically. Sephardic Jews are responsible for the greater number of communal buildings existing to this very day in Istanbul. Sephardic Jews have likewise filled the most important communal functions, including that of chief rabbi, for nearly five centuries.

Many family names of Istanbul Jews recall Spanish cities and provinces, such as Toledano, Mayorkas, Katalan and Adut. Franco, Benveniste and Amarilyo, amongst many others, also indicate Spanish origin.

In addition to these groups, one should consider the Arabic-speaking Jewish families who back in the 19th century moved to Istanbul from the Arab provinces of the Ottoman Empire, such as the Tawashi family of Aleppo, and Jews from Georgia who first settled in eastern Anatolia last century before moving on to Istanbul a few decades ago.

E) Non-Orthodox Jews: Of those Jews who have traditionally rejected Rabbinic authority, the **Karaites** have been the most dominant. Having formed a separate community since 8th-century Babylonia, many members of this sect settled in Byzantine Constantinople. Benjamin de Tudela recorded 500 Karaites in 1176. Their number increased by additional coreligionists resettled by the Ottoman conquerors, most Karaites gathered in the neighborhoods of Hasköy and Karaköy. Separate synagogues observing Karaite rituals were established. The Karaite dead are interred in a separate plot of the Hasköy Jewish cemetery.

The Russian annexation of the Crimean Peninsula in the late 18th century engendered a new wave of immigration that brought many Karaites to the city. The Karaite community of Istanbul never exceeded 1,000 members. They were well integrated in the economic spheres of the city, as indeed they are today.

Unlike their brethren throughout the Middle

East, Turkish Karaites do not claim a Semitic ethnic origin, but instead regard themselves as members of the Turkish people. It is not for nothing that the Karaites are locally dubbed "Turkish Jews". That they are the only Greek-speaking Jews of Istanbul today only serves to emphasize the complexity of their status. Many Karaites bear Russian-sounding names, such as Ilya, indicating their place of origin.

The frequently acrimonious relationship existing between Karaites and Jews throughout the Middle East also prevailed in the Ottoman capital. Not recognized by the State as a separate community until the late 19th century, the Karaite community functioned largely under the authority of Rabbinic Jewry. It is true that many of today's Karaites are independant members of the greater Jewish community; nevertheless, mixed marriages (i.e. Karaite/Rabbinate) have a somewhat problematic status.

Few are the Karaites who frequent the Hasköy synagogue of the Karaite community. Today few are the remaining Karaites who continue to strive for the preservation of a fading heritage (see also "Hasköy").

The Karaites were not the only group to splinter away from Rabbinic Judaism in Israel. One could mention the Khazars, the descendants of the semi-legendary medieval Jewish kingdom on the shores of the Caspian Sea. Samaritan Jews also made their way to Istanbul, transported from Cairo by the Ottomans in 1517. Of these two groups, neither has survived in the city to the present.

F) The Sabbatians (known in Turkish as Dönme): Alongside these Jewish communities of Istanbul exists another, rather more curious sect of Jewish origin. Its formation dates back to that explosion of Messianic longing which swept the entire Jewish people in the 17th century. The self-proclaimed Messiah, **Shabbetai Zevi** (1629-1676), seemed to offer the enthraled Jewish masses the dawn of a new era, the one for which Jews had prayed and yearned for so many millenia.

So vivid were the expectations, so fervent the yearnings, that it was only with the stunning conversion to Islam of this Messiah (1666) that World Jewry woke up to find a shattered Messianic dream.

Yet there were those Jews who refused to abandon hope, seeing in this strange and unexpected development a reflection, a parallel, to all those trials suffered by the Jews of the Iberian Peninsula. According to these Jews, the converted Messiah was forced to conceal his Jewish identity until such time that the moment for revelation should be ripe.

So unshaken was their belief in this Messiah, that around 300 Jewish families from Saloniki converted to Islam in 1683. By the early 20th century some 20,000 members of this sect resided in Saloniki. The descendants of these converts maintained a more or less peaceful coexistence with their rabbinic Jewish neighbors for some 200 years. Political upheavals — such as the 1912-13 Balkan Wars and the 1924 population exchange between Turkey and Greece — forced the members of this sect to make their way to Istanbul.

Re-establishing their accustomed lifestyle and religious ceremonies in the neighborhoods of Nişantaş-Teşvikiye, the refined and highly educated Sabbatians soon became an integral part of Turkish society.

Recognized neither by the chief rabbinate as Jews nor by the more fundamental Islamic circles as full-fledged Muslims, the Sabbatians lead a somewhat isolated life. There are certain temples and burial grounds known locally as the traditional preserves of the Sabbatians (see "Nişantaş" and "Üsküdar").

A veil of mystery enshrouds this sect. Estimates of their numbers vary anywhere from 20,000 to 50,000 people. Only in Istanbul does there still exist a remnant of this religious movement, which once so dramatically changed the destiny of World Jewry. Even though all members of this sect bear typical Islamic names, many of them secretly maintain old Jewish names as well. David Russo, to give one example, was the original name of Cavid Bey, the well-known politician of Sabbatian origin who served as a Minister of Finance in the post-1908 Young Turk government.

Historical circumstances, and first and foremost the mass immigration to other shores, have gone a long way towards softening the friction and conflicts that so often threatened Jewish solidarity in Istanbul. Nowadays, all groups (to the exclusion of the Sabbatians) are united around the elected community leadership. The chief rabbinate and the elected councils represent all sects regardless of origin even though the Ashkenazim, Italians and Karaites maintain separate institutions.

That members of the once disdained local Karaites were recently asked to contribute to the rabbinical community is an action as symbolic as any of the historical rifts that have fallen by the wayside of history.

Jewish houses in Kuzguncuk

JEWISH SITES IN ISTANBUL

✡ = areas with major Jewish sites
A = synagogue (27)
B = cemetery (9)
C = communal institutions (schools, clubs, hospitals, etc.) (12)
D = other Jewish-related sites (museums, public buildings, etc.) (11)

Total Jewish sites marked on this map: 59

Eyüp

B ✡ A C A
Hasköy
D ✡

B C
A *Balat* D ✡
✡ A A A
A A

D

Old City

D

A
Bakırköy

MARMARA SEA

GOLDEN HORN

Burg

Hey

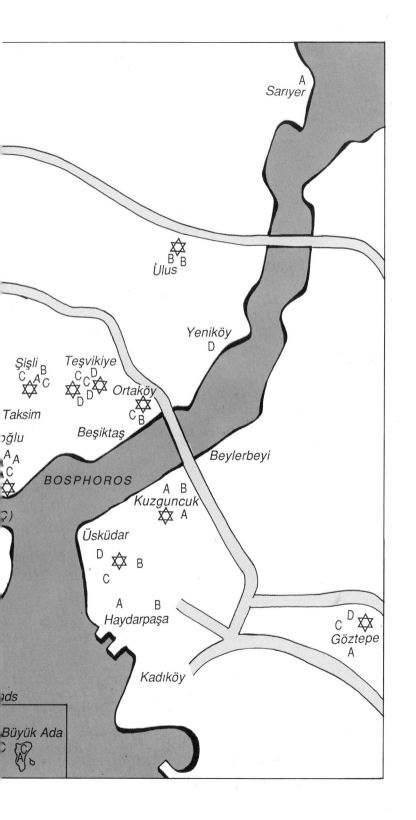

TOPOGRAPHY AND ORIENTATION

The Jews of Istanbul have always resided in neighborhoods side by side with Muslim and Christian neighbors. Though an occasional corner of some neighborhoods may have been considered as strictly Jewish, the majority of dwellings house people of all persuasions. Such is it the case in Istanbul today.

Yet in the early Ottoman period the neighborhoods of Istanbul were organized in a different fashion. During the 15th-17th centuries, certain neighborhoods, (Balat, Hasköy and Kuzguncuk) were so predominantly Jewish that they were locally recognized as "Jewish Neighborhoods" (*Yahudi Mahallesi*). The 19th century saw a shift to the district of Galata as the major focus of Jewish life. All in all, Jews have lived in most of the major neighborhoods of the city. Only such neighborhoods with strong Muslim majorities as Fatih and Üsküdar, have rarely housed a Jewish population of any size.

The neighborhoods that did witness a large influx of Jews were not by any means European-style "ghettoes". Jews tended to flock together for reasons both social and religious, but there was never any pressure, either political or governmental, to isolate their presence in the city.

The migration from neighborhood to neighborhood was often the result of natural disasters such as fires, epidemics and earthquakes. Yet the search for better living conditions often governed the population shifts: only the poorer and less fortunate Jews were being left behind in the old neighborhoods.

The first Jewish settlement in Ottoman Istanbul was nestled in the Eminönü-Sirkeci harbor of the old city. Immediately following the Ottoman conquest, the Sultan designated this region as a focus for Jewish settlement. And indeed, the neighborhood served as a magnet for Jewish immigrants from the provinces, as well as those former Jewish residents of Pera fleeing battles that ultimately toppled the Byzantine Empire.

The neighborhoods of Balat and Hasköy sprang up during the 16th century on either side of the Golden Horn. That these neighborhoods evolved as great centers of Jewish life can be seen by the various community buildings that exist to this very day.

The 19th century was an era of change for many Jews. The old and overcrowded neighborhoods were gradually emptied of their Jewish residents as these thronged to the modern districts of Galata and Pera. Such was the impact of this population flow that Galata became the nerve center of the entire Jewish community. Amongst institutions relocated in this district we find the chief rabbinate. Other central organizations related to administration and communal life first crystallized in this neighborhood.

Lighting candles at Hanuka

Modern though the district of Galata certainly was, this nevertheless did not prevent Jews as time passed, from seeking the even newer neighborhoods of Şişli, Nişantaş and their environs. By the mid 20th century this area contained over half of Istanbul Jewry. Whereas communal and religious affairs continued to be conducted in the Galata area, cultural life flourished around the Şişli-based cultural centers.

Moving now to the Bosphorus region, we find the two old neighborhoods of Ortaköy and Kuzguncuk situated on either shore of the strait, one proudly facing the other. Traces of past magnificence still bear witness to these once important Jewish centers.

North of Ortaköy, along the European shores of the Bosphorus, only a few sites of Jewish significance still remain in Arnavutköy and Yeniköy. Two relatively new Jewish cemeteries are located in the modern neighborhood of Ulus, a recent focus for Jewish home-owners.

Kuzguncuk is not the only Jewish landmark on the Asian side of Istanbul. Not far from this neighborhood are located the Haydarpaşa Synagogue and the Sabbatian cemetery of Üsküdar. The recent development of Asian Istanbul has attracted many Jews to shores which formerly housed only a summer community.

In summary, a general estimate would place some 60% of today's Istanbul Jewry on the European side of the city, the remaining 40% in the new Asian suburbs surrounding Göztepe. Few Jews remain in the time-worn but still colorful old neighborhoods of Galata, Ortaköy and Kuzguncuk. A growing Jewish community has lately assembled in the neighborhood of Bakırköy. With the exception of some 100 inhabitants of the Hasköy Jewish Old-Age Home, no Jews at all remain on either shore of the Golden Horn.

Before embarking on a detailed description of each neighborhood and its major Jewish sites, it is best to offer some general tips. While many well-known Jewish sites are easily located, others — mostly in the older part of the city — are less accessible. In such cases, the most intrepid visitor, armed with the most detailed map, will often find himself with no resort but to ask for the help of passer-bys. The glossary attached to this guide should be of special assistance when conversing with local residents.

It is often necessary to arrange special appointments when visiting certain sites, as some of the most important places have been forced to remain closed due to security reasons or lack of personnel. Most synagogues hold daily services, both in the mornings and in the evenings. Nearly all are open to the public on holidays and special occasions.

Security is enforced by sophisticated means. Special permission is required for those who wish entry to the Chief Rabbinate as well as to all other community institutions. It is due to such consideration of security that the visitor is best advised to request permission before taking pictures.

Several synagogues are open only in certain seasons: thus, the synagogues on the Princes' Islands and the Beth-Ya'akov synagogue of Kuzguncuk are frequented only in summer (June to September). The Balat synagogue of Yanbol is open only on the holiday of Succot.

Hotels and restaurants are a rarity in older neighborhoods such as Balat; modern well-equipped ones are non-existent. In other neigborhoods, such as Hasköy and Kuzguncuk, some of the most attractive tourist sites are located on hilltops, but adequate public transportation is not always available, and even taxis are not always easy to come by.

A tour of the Jewish sites of Istanbul should take into consideration not only Jewish festivals, but national and Islamic holidays as well.

Istanbul has been blessed with a unique geography. It is for this reason that a neighborhood appearing no larger than a pin on the map will reveal itself as a sprawling snarl of intricate lanes and hilly terrain. Adding to this the difficulty of finding many a historical site, it is accordingly recommended to plan one's itinerary with a good measure of realism.

A complex web of inter-ethnic relations has always been the hallmark of Istanbul. It is for this reason that the visitor in search of the Jewish heritage must remain sensitive to the mutual flow of inter-religious influence. Sites which may appear quite outside the domain of Judaism may indeed have played a vital role in the life of Istanbul Jewry.

The Galata Tower

For a comprehensive tour of Jewish sites, Istanbul is best divided into five separate areas:

1) The Southern Shore of the Golden Horn: Sirkeci-Eminönü-Balat, including the recommended neighborhoods of Fener and Eyüp. The Jewish neighborhood of Balat would be the focus of this tour; visits to the great local non-Jewish sites such as Hagia Sophia are best left to a separate tour.

2) The Northern Shore of the Golden Horn: Hasköy-Kasımpaşa. A visit to this neighborhood should require no more than a few hours; the decay of time and history has eroded nearly all sites that once testified to the presence of a bustling and prosperous center. Thus, it is best to consider the following two possibilities: (A) A combined tour of Hasköy with Balat, crossing the Golden Horn by boat. (B) A combined tour of Hasköy with Galata, passing through Kasımpaşa.

3) The Beyoğlu District: Galata-Karaköy-Şişhane-Tünel-İstiklal Caddesi. This is the sector most richly endowed with Jewish sites, most of which are grouped in the area around the Galata Tower. Several non-Jewish sites intertwined with Jewish history, such as the Pera Palace Hotel, have been included in this tour.

4) The European Shore of the Bosphorus: Ortaköy-Şişli-Nişantaş. Ortaköy would be the major attraction of this tour along with the Yeniköy synagogue. From this vantage point the Jewish sites of Şişli, Nişantaş and Ulus, as well as the Sabbatian center of Teşvikiye, are easily reached. Less than one day devoted to this district would surely deprive the visitor of many interesting points.

5) The Asian Shore of the Bosphorus: Kuzguncuk-Üsküdar-Haydarpaşa-Göztepe. Kuzguncuk certainly forms the major focus of this tour. From Kuzguncuk one could proceed along the Bosphorus to Üsküdar (Dönme cemetery), Haydarpaşa (synagogue), and the Jewish centers of Göztepe. This tour could wind up in Bostancı, from which depart regular boat services to Istanbul and the Princes' Islands.

No guidebook can truly present the vast panorama that makes up a city such as Istanbul. This tour guide of Jewish sites of Istanbul is the first of its kind, and though much care and study have been devoted to it, it can make no sweeping claims to comprehensiveness. Yet perhaps it is better this way, because in the last resort it is imagination and a sense of adventure that will not only present the city to the eyes of the newcomer, but also implant its image unto his heart.

A wanderer in the streets of Istanbul can make many fascinating discoveries on his own, but for this task he must be well prepared. The following will provide valuable tips for discovering the Jewish facets of Istanbul.

Public and private homes formerly housing Jewish residents are characterized by certain traditional Jewish symbols such as *Mezuza* and the Star of David. Commemorative dates in either Hebrew or Arabic figures are often embossed in the lintel above the doorway. The date can be calculated by adding the sum of 1240 to the number to the last three digits of the four digit number engraved on the house: (5)659 + 1240 = 1899. While on the subject of math, the number 18, traditionally associated with the Hebrew word for life, is best kept in mind. Row houses found 18 to a row are likely to be connected with Jewish heritage. The most famous example is the row houses of Ortaköy.

One sure way of locating Jewish buildings is by finding the synagogue. The special decorative features of Jewish architecture render these houses easily identifiable. The jutting balconies and the bay windows are the hallmarks of these houses often built on stone foundations with wooden upper stories. The visitor should not be surprised when he comes across these homes from one neighborhood to the other. So attached were the Jews to this style of architecture that even the removal to new neighborhoods would entail the building of such houses, smack in the middle of their new surroundings. Such is the case in Haydarpaşa: Jews moving there from the vicinity of Kuzguncuk in the late 19th century built a number of such houses around their local synagogue.

The architecture of a building is often not only a measure of taste, but also the reflection of the winds blowing in from abroad during all periods of Ottoman history. Whereas synagogues of the early Ottoman period were often modeled after the courtyard architecture of the Iberian peninsula, schools of the late Ottoman period tended to follow French fashions of taste. The Alliance Israélite Universelle schools are a monument to contemporary French architecture.

But in the hustle and bustle of everyday life such symbols of Jewish life are not always as prominent as they appear on the printed page. Buildings are often crumbling if not totally decayed, and an engraved date may be half eroded by time. In short, it takes a fresh eye and a willing heart to lure an ancient Jewish heritage from its often dusty and obscure background.

A Jewish house in Galata

MAJOR JEWISH NEIGHBORHOODS

The Southern Shore of the Golden Horn

Eminönü-Sirkeci

General orientation: The following area is accessible from any direction and any part of the city. To reach Eminönü, the starting point of this tour: (1) by boat from the stations on either sides of the Bosphorus; (2) by train to the Sirkeci train station; (3) by bus from any city bus stop; (4) via the Tünel and Galata Bridge.

A major embarkation and disembarkation point for most maritime lines of the entire country, and a central commercial district, this area is one of the most bustling of Istanbul. This is a major starting point for many tourists, and one is best advised to take into account the crowded conditions and congested traffic when planning one's tour.

It is also the ideal starting point for the visitor intent upon Jewish history, since Eminönü harbor formed the very first Jewish settlement following the 1453 Ottoman conquest. Eminönü was designated a Jewish quarter almost as soon as the dust of the battle settled down, and Sultan Mehmet the Conqueror was most anxious to resettle the depopulated areas of the city. It was due to this policy that former Jewish residents not only returned to Istanbul but were joined by other Jews from newly conquered territories, Rabbinate and Karaite Jews alike.

The erection of the **New Mosque (Yeni Cami)** in 1597 brought an end to this Jewish presence. Forbidden to reside in the proximity of Islamic religious sites, the Jews moved to other neighborhoods on either side of the Golden Horn. This process happened again and again until hardly a single Jew was to be found in this quarter of the old city.

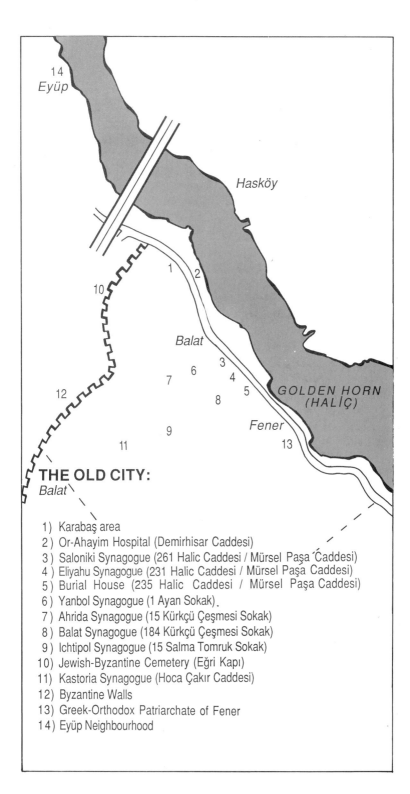

THE OLD CITY:
Balat

1) Karabaş area
2) Or-Ahayim Hospital (Demirhisar Caddesi)
3) Saloniki Synagogue (261 Halic Caddesi / Mürsel Paşa Caddesi)
4) Eliyahu Synagogue (231 Halic Caddesi / Mürsel Paşa Caddesi)
5) Burial House (235 Halic Caddesi / Mürsel Paşa Caddesi)
6) Yanbol Synagogue (1 Ayan Sokak)
7) Ahrida Synagogue (15 Kürkçü Çeşmesi Sokak)
8) Balat Synagogue (184 Kürkçü Çeşmesi Sokak)
9) Ichtipol Synagogue (15 Salma Tomruk Sokak)
10) Jewish-Byzantine Cemetery (Eğri Kapı)
11) Kastoria Synagogue (Hoca Çakır Caddesi)
12) Byzantine Walls
13) Greek-Orthodox Patriarchate of Fener
14) Eyüp Neighbourhood

It is due to this same process that the visitor of today will find only very few vestiges of Jewish history, often in the most unexpected places. A Star of David engraved above the doorway of the Yeni Cami (half hidden underneath the office sign of Ayvalık Vakıflar) is the last remnant of a Karaite synagogue traditionally believed to have been situated there. This synagogue, like all other Karaite synagogues, would have been located underground. Yet a word of caution is in order. The Star of David has not always been a necessarily Jewish symbol. For example, the Star of David that figures so prominently on the mosque on Fuad Paşa Sokak No. 39 (not far from the Süleymaniye mosque) can have no connection with a Jewish past.

All the Islamic prohibitions notwithstanding, the late Ottoman period witnessed a steady trickle of Jewish merchants and businessmen to this area. Thus do Ottoman sources reveal a presence of some 5,000 local Jews, some of whom resided in neighborhoods known for their strict Islamic character, such as Fatih.

The **Sirkeci synagogue,** just behind the Sirkeci train station at 1, İstasyon Arkası Sokak (tel: 5133043), was established for this community. Many Jewish refugees arriving from eastern Europe and the Balkans around the turn of the century were amongst those who attended services in this synagogue. The beautifully appointed train station (inaugurated in 1875) occupies an interesting niche in local Jewish history. Many of these refugees arrived via this train station. A Ladino song on the lips of many (*Los Kamino de Sirkeci*) commemorates a group of refugees from European Turkey who escaped German-incited riots in the mid-1930s.

Another wave of refugees settled in the adjoining neighborhood of **Bakırköy**, establishing a synagogue used to this very day (Cumhuriyet Sokak, Zeytinlik Mahallesi, Tel: 5425102). Bakırköy served as another temporary waystation for Sabbatian refugees from Saloniki, during the Turkish-Greek population exchange in 1924. At first settling in abandoned Greek homes, they later joined their co-religionists in the

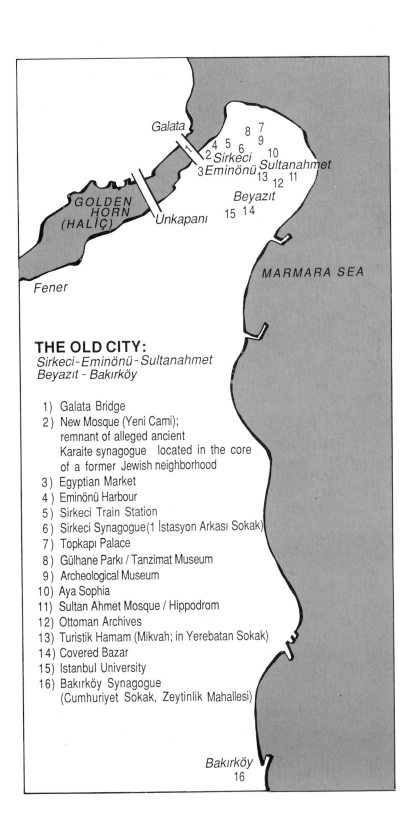

THE OLD CITY:
*Sirkeci-Eminönü-Sultanahmet
Beyazıt - Bakırköy*

1) Galata Bridge
2) New Mosque (Yeni Cami);
   remnant of alleged ancient
   Karaite synagogue located in the core
   of a former Jewish neighborhood
3) Egyptian Market
4) Eminönü Harbour
5) Sirkeci Train Station
6) Sirkeci Synagogue(1 İstasyon Arkası Sokak)
7) Topkapı Palace
8) Gülhane Parkı / Tanzimat Museum
9) Archeological Museum
10) Aya Sophia
11) Sultan Ahmet Mosque / Hippodrom
12) Ottoman Archives
13) Turistik Hamam (Mikvah; in Yerebatan Sokak)
14) Covered Bazar
15) Istanbul University
16) Bakırköy Synagogue
    (Cumhuriyet Sokak, Zeytinlik Mahallesi)

neighborhood of Teşvikiye. A substantial number of Jews have lately moved to this area, attracted by its rapid development.

Although not of strict Jewish interest, there are a number of well-known sites not without interest in this tour.

The **Topkapı Palace:** This palace served as the imperial residence and seat of government between the 15th and the mid-19th centuries. It was from this palace that the decree first welcoming the Spanish Jews to Ottoman shores was issued. The tower rising majestically above the palace walls, commonly known as the Tower of Justice, came to symbolize the principles that governed the Sultan's Jewish policy over the centuries. From behind this tower, unseen but all-powerful, the Sultan dispensed justice to his subjects.

The palace gardens saw many an impressive ceremony inaugurating important imperial policies. No policy could have been more momentous for Ottoman Jews than the sweeping Tanzimat (reforms) of 1839. For this occasion the Rose Gardens of Gülhane Park were used. The site on which Sultan Abdülmecit granted equality to his non-Muslim subjects now serves as the **Museum of the Tanzimat.** This museum contains an interesting collection transferred there from Yıldız Palace some 20 years ago: original edicts, portraits of leading dignitaries of the Tanzimat, oil paintings depicting the ceremony, and most intriguing of all — the ballot box used for the first Ottoman Parliament. The museum is located in the center of Gülhane Park and is open daily 9:00-17:00.

The **Archaeological Museum** next to the palace contains several exhibits related to Jewish history. Two displays brought by the Ottomans from the land of Israel in the early 20th century are of special interest: The first floor contains the "Gezer Inscription", a plaque chiselled in the 10th century B.C. describing the agricultural activities of ancient Canaan. The famous "Shiloah Inscription" describes the excitement of the workers who tunneled their way through to the spring outside of Jerusalem's walls, in the tumultuous days of King Hezekiah. Open every day except Monday 9:00-17:00.

The ancient Byzantine forum is situated not far from the Topkapı Palace. Though separated by a mere few steps, the distance between the two cultures could not be greater for the Jews. Persecution, expulsion, and forced conversion had been the Jewish lot in Byzantine times, and the Ottoman conquest was thereby eagerly welcomed.

Under the new order, Jews were immediately granted equal economic opportunities. The **Grand Covered Bazaar**, located in the nearby Beyazıt district, has been humming with Jewish activity ever since its founding in the 15th century. Should a visitor from those early days happen to chance by this bazaar, he would probably not be in the least surprised by the number of Jewish-owned shops.

There are three additional attractions in the vicinity of the Grand Bazaar: The charming **Turistik Hamam**, situated at the corner of Ankara Sokak, and Yerebatan Sokak (Sultanahmet), is used by the Jewish women of the community as a *Mikvah* (ritual bath).

Just opposite the Bazaar are situated the **Ottoman Archives**, rich in information concerning Ottoman Jewry. Holding sway as they did over approximately half a million Jews, the Ottomans' archives present a veritable treasure trove of information on Jewish history. Documents recording everything from social phenomena to the economic situation, are available here in profusion, enabling the researcher to piece together a fascinating picture of daily Jewish life in old Istanbul.

Istanbul University, established in the 19th century as the first institution for higher education in the Ottoman Empire, stands not far from the Archives. The two most famous Jews to have attended this university — which has enrolled Jews ever since it first opened its doors — were undoubtedly **David Ben-Gurion** (first prime minister of the State of Israel) and **Yitzak Ben-Zvi** (the second president of Israel).

Both were young law students in the pre-WWI years, eager to participate in the fervent Zionistic activity of the Ottoman capital. These activities came to an abrupt end with the dissolution of the Ottoman Empire following the war. Both men were to make good use of the experience and knowledge gained during their student years: Ben-Gurion based much of his administrative and judicial measures on Ottoman patterns; Ben-Zvi was later to become a distinguished scholar of eastern Jewry.

Moving westward towards the Golden Horn, the visitor will find himself in the very heart of Jewish Istanbul. The two neighborhoods of Balat and Hasköy eventually replaced the Eminönü-Sirkeci district in the 17th century as the focus of Jewish life.

The Castoria synagogue

Balat

General orientation: The neighborhood of Balat is located on the southern shore of the Golden Horn between the neighborhoods of Fener and Eyüp. To reach the neighborhood one can either take a boat from Üsküdar via Kasımpaşa or a bus/taxi from Eminönü. A more picturesque route is by bus or taxi along the Golden Horn.

The tour to the Balat area might be combined with a tour of either the Eminönü or the Hasköy neighborhood. With few exceptions, most sites included in this tour are situated in a compact area near the shore of the Golden Horn. This tour is accordingly particularly enjoyable on foot.

Strolling through this quarter is a treat for all the senses. Ancient and dilapidated though Balat is, life here seems to offer a particularly rich tapestry of color. Indeed, the entranced visitor might easily believe himself to have found the Istanbul of his imagination.

Not a small part of this vibrant image is due to the incessant throng of people of all ethnic and religious origins. Churches, synagogues and mosques huddle one next to the other; Greeks, Armenians and Turks stroll side by side. Whether the result of deliberate urban planning or the outcome of historical processes, this most Jewish of quarters finds itself geographically located between the most pious Islamic and Greek-Orthodox neighborhoods of Istanbul: Eyüp with its holy Islamic shrines and Fener, the seat of the Oecumenical patriarchate is.

Balat has been the core of the Jewish presence in Istanbul for over five centuries. A small Jewish settlement had gathered there already in the Byzantine period as witnessed by several old synagogues as well as scattered gravestones bearing Romaniot names found in the vicinity of the nearby ancient Byzantine walls. Nearly all major events pertaining to the Jewish community of Ottoman Istanbul during its heyday occurred in this neigborhood. It was only in the 18th and 19th centuries that Balat declined in importance as Jews migrated to newer neighborhoods. Fire and earthquake contributed to the gradual decline. So steady was the stream of migration that hardly any Jew has resided there in nearly three decades.

The story of Jewish Balat begins to unfold shortly after the Ottoman conquest of Istanbul. Jews settling there under the encouraging policy of the government saw their number augmented by waves of Spanish refugees following the expulsion of 1492. It was, in fact, these Spanish newcomers who gave Balat its impetus.

The Jewish population of Balat overflowed into the surrounding northern neighborhoods of Ayvan Saray and Tekfur Saray, and into the Fener and Aya Kapı neighborhoods in the south. In the 17th century we find nearly 2,000 Jewish families in this area.

The depredations of time notwithstanding, there remain not a few important sites of extremely well-preserved appearance. The various processes of renovation have not robbed these buildings of their patina of time and authenticity. The relatively modern Jewish dates engraved on the buildings should not be the occasion for dismay; these dates merely indicate the latest renovation.

Renovation is an ongoing process. With the festivities celebrating the 500th anniversary of Jewish immigration from Spain to Turkey, renovation designed to restore the glory of major Jewish edifices is proceeding at a rapid pace.

A tour to Balat will reveal not only the richness of Jewish life, but the very structure of the community itself. It was here that the division of Jews based on various social and geographical aspects first crystallized. Romaniot, Sephardic, Ashkenazi, Italian: all had their established congregations and rituals of life in Balat. Amongst all the factors governing a Jew's place in the local congregation, none was more important than the city from which he hailed.

Nearly every congregation was named after a city left behind in the Iberian Peninsula or in the Balkan countries. Even today, synagogues in Balat bear silent witness to these far away lands. Such is the case with the synagogues of Saloniki, Castoria, and Ichtipol (İştip), the founders of which had emigrated from Macedonia.

Family tradition and prized local customs were thereby preserved by the transported congregations, but such preservation was achieved at the expense of a greater social solidaritiy. And even the jealously maintained tradition proved to be only temporary. The Jews who eventually thronged to the new neighborhoods allowed these divisions to fall into abeyance.

The Jewish residences were divided into three major areas: (1) The shores of the Golden Horn attracted numerous residents, especially those who made a living from the sea. A large part of this area, known as **Karabaş,** was destroyed by the Municipality some 10 years ago and replaced by a park. Of the few Jewish sites remaining, the local Jewish hospital is the most important. The gates of two old and crumbling synagogues alongside the Haliç Caddesi, are the last visible evidence of the once bustling artery of a busy Jewish center; (2) the crumbling **Ichtipol synagogue** is all that remains of the once thriving Jewish community that was perched on the slopes of the hill rising from the Golden Horn; (3) the third area, located geographically between the two above areas, contains many of the major Jewish attractions of the neighborhood. It was here, alongside Eski Kasap Sokak, that the residents would gather for all community functions and festivities.

Kürkçü Çeşmesi Sokak is a fine starting point for our tour. Colorful though the street is, its present, somewhat dowdy appearance hides the fact that lovely homes built around inner courtyards once housed a numerous Jewish population here. Many of the families lived in the rear part of the house, the front half being maintained as a shop or small workshop. No village or town could offer a scene more poignantly Jewish than the one that unfolded every

Sabbath and holiday: Jews of all age and rank, dressed in their finest, would fill the street with happy chatter in a variety of languages spiced heavily with Ladino.

That Jews lived a contented and fulfilling Jewish life without fear is evident to this very day from the Stars of David and Hebrew dates incised prominently into the façades of their home. See, for example, the balcony on the house at no. 68; the Hebrew date is 5680 (1920). Another example is the house with Stars of David embossed on the façade.

At its peak, this street housed many communal institutions that served Istanbul Jewry in general. Up until some 30 years ago the **Hahamhane Community Center,** located in the middle of this neighborhood, was a busy and cheerful meeting place. Such a center served for various purposes, such as celebrations of religious holidays, weddings and the site of the local rabbinical court and sometimes even a jail. Oldtimers still recall the many festivities and religious ceremonies that once filled this center. A conflagration some 30 years ago put an end to all these activities. A movie theater subsequently took its place, followed by an apartment building.

This street also boasted numerous educational facilities. Traditional Yeshivas mingled with the newer schools built in the 19th century. The synagogues were by far the most impressive of all Jewish buildings on this street. Very few remain; the gate located at no. 184 is all that survives of one such synagogue. As engraved on its gate (in Hebrew and Ottoman script), this synagogue was erected (most probably restored) in 1876 (5636) and served the "Balat Holy Congregation".

Balat has no more impressive site than the **Ahrida synagogue**, at 15 Kürkçü Çeşmesi Sokak. Named after the Macedonian city of Ohrid (rose), this synagogue is the oldest and most beautiful of Istanbul. According to local tradition it was built by Romaniot Jews in the 15th century. Constructed prior to the Ottoman conquest, the synagogue was permitted to function by imperial decree.

Of all the major events that took place within this synagogue, none could have been more epoch-making than the appearance of **Shabbetai Zevi** one Saturday afternoon. For it was at this time that the self-proclaimed Messiah announced his mission directly to the local community, a mission that was to have such devastating effects for World Jewry. The immediate effect upon the congregation was just as overwhelming, and the religious leadership united to forcibly excommunicate and banish Shabbetai Zevi from the city. Renovated at various times throughout the centuries, this synagogue underwent its last major overhaul in 1955. A memorial plaque inside the synagogue bears a moving inscription describing the joy of those Jews who participated in its restoration. Almost breathtaking in its magnificence, the synagogue can seat some 500 worshippers. An unusual detail of this synagogue is the raised platform in the shape of a "Noah's Ark" situated in the center of the hall. The Holy Ark, enclosed by rich tapestries (*parochet*), conceals rare and valuable holy scrolls.

The Ahrida synagogue in Balat

The offices located in the courtyard are lined with photographs depicting memorable moments in the life of the congregation. **Rabbi Albert Bahar** presides with energy and dignity over this most venerable of synagogues. A study house (*Beit Midrash*) is just across the courtyard, serving the handful of worshippers who gather for the daily prayers.

Saturday prayers attract a somewhat larger crowd of some 30 Jews who arrive from all parts of Istanbul. Thrice yearly the synagogue is filled to bursting with Jewish worshippers; the festivals of Rosh Hashana, Passover, and Purim offer a particularly happy scene: young children of the congregation stage a lively Purim play, with bright costumes and songs.

In conjunction with the 500th anniversary celebrations, the Ahrida synagogue has been the subject of a comprehensive restoration conducted under the supervision of the well-known Turkish architect Hüsrev Talya. The final shape of the synagogue will follow the late 17th-century Baroque style restoration.

The nearby **Yanbol synagogue,** located close by at 1, Ayan Sokak is traditionally opened once a year in order to hold the festivities of Succoth. It is assumed that this synagogue, which is named after the Bulgarian city of Yanbol, already existed in Byzantine times. A fading inscription on the lintel of the impressive doorway records the date of the most recent renovation: 1875 (Hebrew date 5635). The well-appointed interior of the synagogue presents a memorable sight; the synagogue can seat some three hundred worshippers.

The Ahrida and Yanbol synagogues are the only remaining active synagogues in Balat. Just behind these synagogues, and perched on a hillside, the **Ichtipol synagogue,** named after the Macedonian city of Iştip, has a forlorn and desolate air; for over twenty years its walls have been closed to worshippers. Located at 62, Salma Tomruk Sokak it was founded in the early Ottoman period and had its most recent renovation in 1903, as we learn from an inscription.

This decrepit wooden synagogue has little to offer the curious visitor behind its encircling wall. Just across the street stands a row of sumptuous houses. Formerly inhabited by Jews, they are now abandoned.

Not far from there, we come across the remnants of the **Castoria synagogue** (132, Hoca Çakır Sokak) adjacent to the Byzantine wall. The name Castoria (in Hebrew) and the date 5653 (1893) are inscribed on the synagogue's gate, the only part left intact; this synagogue — whose founders settled in this area following their departure from the Macedonian city of Castoria after the capture of Istanbul by the Ottomans — was active until its destruction in 1937. Though ruined, one can still see the remnants of the Old Holy Ark as well as scattered Hebrew-inscribed grave stones

Descending the hill back to the shores of the Golden Horn, we have now reached our third and final group of sites. Along the shore-road (Haliç Caddesi) and located side by side are three crumbling old buildings: (1) A once-ornate gate announces the **"Saloniki Synagogue"**, although nothing else remains. The date on the gate is 1926 (5686); a synagogue of this name is known to have existed in Balat since the 16th century, sheltering a congregation whose members were transferred from Saloniki to Istanbul by Sultan Mehmed the Conqueror. (2) Not far (at no. 2) is the lonely gate of another ruined synagogue, the **Eliyahu synagogue,** as is revealed by a minute inscription. This synagogue was renovated in 1896. (3) Adjacent to the Eliyahu synagogue is another building which served as the local **Burial Society** up until some thirty years ago. The building now houses a garage; the owners relate that until about twenty years ago two elderly Jewish ladies lingered on here.

We have now reached the last site of Jewish interest. Along this same shore-road in the direction of Eyüp stands the **Or-Ahayim Hospital,** the first and only Jewish hospital of Istanbul. This hospital was established in 1899 — as indicated by the inscription on the gate. The dining-hall contains an imperial decree on its walls and a portrait of the founding physicians of the institution.

Built from the donations of Jews both local and foreign, this hospital was inaugurated with much festivity. The hospital was reinforced by a generous donation of the **Kadoori** family from Irak in 1922; the synagogue located inside the hospital is named after this philanthropic family. This tiny synagogue serves the local community to this day. A memorial service is held yearly for the distinguished historian and member of the Turkish parliament, **Abraham Galante,** who passed away on August 19th, 1961.

Though constructed for and by Jews, the hospital now serves a largely non-Jewish population; scarcely half a *minyan* of six or seven Jews are available amongst the patients at prayer time. This fact, when added to the half-ruined synagogues and lonely gates of abandoned buildings so common throughout Balat, bears silent but eloquent testimony to the disintegration of a once-proud Jewish neighborhood.

Finally we come across the remains of Istanbul's oldest Jewish graveyard adjacent to the city walls close by at **Eğri Kapı.** No longer functioning as a burial place since 1939, this cemetery originally served the Jewish community of Byzantine Constantinople. Accordingly, Istanbul's first chief rabbi under Ottoman rule, **Moses Capsali** (d. 1499), was buried here. Since 1939, local Jews bury their deads at the Hasköy Jewish cemetery. Gravestones bearing Jewish names of Byzantine origin which were discovered several years ago in this place were transferred to the Jewish cemetery at the request of the chief rabbinate.

The Northern Shore of the Golden Horn
Hasköy-Kasımpaşa

General Orientation: A rather isolated neighborhood, Hasköy is situated on the northern shore of the Golden Horn, just across the bay from Balat. Not easily accessible by public transportation, the area can be reached either by boat from Balat boat station or by land (1) from Galata via the neighborhood of Kasımpaşa; (2) from Şişli via the highway encompassing the city. But no matter which way you choose, the unique terrain will require quite a bit of walking.

During the early Ottoman period, Hasköy and Balat were the traditional Jewish neighborhoods par excellence. Yet Hasköy retained its own character, clearly distinguished from its sister neighborhood: (1) the level of affluence was generally higher; (2) educational institutions were somewhat better developed; and (3) it was the center of Karaite activity.

Hasköy was one of the major neighborhoods designated by the Ottoman government for Jewish settlement in the early years following the conquest. Jews arriving from far and wide throughout the vast Ottoman realm received generous financial encouragement from the authorities.

Within a short period of time, Hasköy developed into a teeming conflux of Jews from regions the world over. Romaniot Jews from the recently conquered Balkan territories were resettled in this neighborhood. A group of Jews arriving from Frankfurt in 1483 immediately set up an Ashkenazi community. Many of the arriving Spanish refugees — amongst them some of the most prominent figures of Spanish Jewry — re-established themselves in Hasköy.

The famous 17th-century Turkish traveller **Evliya Çelebi** wrote of a community 11,000-strong, inhabiting every corner of the neighborhood. Çelebi records some 3,000 affluent Jewish homes, many of which commanded a fine view from their situation along the Golden Horn. 18th-century maps indicate that Hasköy was populated predominantly by Jews, with smaller Greek and Armenian communities. But this majority was eventually to dwindle; another traveller, arriving around the turn of the 20th century, found that the local Jewish community numbered but 20,000 of the total 80,000 Jews in Istanbul.

The story of Hasköy is in fact the story of the Golden Age of Istanbul Jewry. Under the charismatic leadership of Jews such as **Moshe Hamon,** personal physician and advisor to **Sultan Mehmed the Conqueror,** it was here in this neighborhood that the timeless character of the Jewish community first crystallized.

No neighborhood was more blessed than Hasköy with Jewish educational and cultural facilities. In view of this tradition, it is not surprising that the first Hebrew printing presses in Istanbul were established in Hasköy. From the very first years, wealthy Jewish dignitaries vied with one another for the privilege of founding educational institutions. Such, for example, was the magnificent "Gvira Yeshiva" founded by **Don Joseph Nasi** in honor of his famous and nearly legendary aunt **Dona Gracia**.

However this tradition may have faded over the centuries and the 19th century saw a renaissance of Jewish education in Hasköy. Even after Galata developed as the leading modern district of the city, the tradition of academic excellence continued its flourishing existence in this venerable neighborhood.

Some of the most modern and progressive educational institutions were established in Hasköy: None was more famous than the **Camondo Institute** (1858-1889), openly recognized as the best Jewish school in the capital. The only school to offer a European standard curriculum, its courses were conducted in French, Turkish, Hebrew and Greek. Over 120 Jewish youths annually benefitted from these well-equipped facilities; an additional 30 boys received training as tailors and shoemakers in the adjoining vocational school.

A rabbinical college with a capacity of 132 male pupils formed another branch of this school. All three branches of the Institute were maintained at the sole expense of Camondo. The Institute was obviously affected by the fate of its founding benefactor; it was only thanks to the generosity of several other wealthy Jews that the Institute continued to function long after the Camondo family was compelled to flee Istanbul.

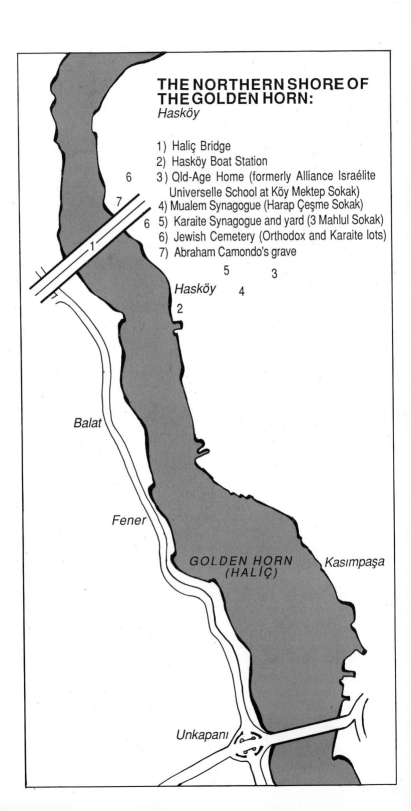

THE NORTHERN SHORE OF THE GOLDEN HORN:
Hasköy

1) Haliç Bridge
2) Hasköy Boat Station
3) Old-Age Home (formerly Alliance Israélite Universelle School at Köy Mektep Sokak)
4) Mualem Synagogue (Harap Çeşme Sokak)
5) Karaite Synagogue and yard (3 Mahlul Sokak)
6) Jewish Cemetery (Orthodox and Karaite lots)
7) Abraham Camondo's grave

Hasköy

Balat

Fener

*GOLDEN HORN
(HALİÇ)*

Kasımpaşa

Unkapanı

Abraham Camondo, the honorary chairman of the regional Alliance Israélite Universelle (AIU), was also the driving force behind the establishment of the AIU school in Hasköy. A sumptuous building constructed in 1899 housed this school.

In 1955, the AIU building was chosen for the newly established rabbinical seminary of Istanbul. An elementary school continued to function in the very building up until 1962. This was the only rabbinical seminary serving the Jews of the region since the rabbinical seminary of Rhodes had been closed down by the Italian authorities. Chief Rabbi **David Asseo,** himself a graduate of the Rhodes seminary and the present chief rabbi of Turkey, served as the first head of the seminary. The second and the last director of the seminary was Rabbi **Elijahu Cohen**. Most contemporary Turkish and regional rabbis have received their training in this seminary. In 1963, it was transferred to Karaköy where it existed up to its final closure in the late 1960's.

Available to neighborhood residents were numerous synagogues, only two of which still remain. The Rabbinical **Mualem synagogue** of Harap Çeşme Sokak is closed during most of the year and its deteriorating interior reflects its declining use. The Hebrew inscription on the half-ruined gate still clearly proclaims the date 1734. The interested visitor can view the synagogue by enlisting the aid of the elderly doorkeeper who lives next door.

The vibrant **Karaite synagogue** presents a study in contrast. Karaites had settled in Hasköy already in the early Ottoman period. Following the Russian conquest of the Crimean Peninsula in the late 19th century and the flight of many of its Karaite residents to Istanbul, Hasköy became the undisputed centre of Karaism in the Balkan region.

The local Karaites resided in the vicinity of their synagogue, located at 3, Mahlul Sokak. This synagogue, named "Bnai Mikra", underwent a series of restorations following the toll of fires and earthquakes. The last major renovation was undertaken in the late 19th century with the help of donations by World Karaite Jewry. Just like every other Karaite synagogue, this one too is built underground. Curious as this may seem, the explanation lies in the Biblical phrase: "From the depths I called to thee, O Lord" (Psalms 130:1). The interior is furnished in typical Karaite fashion: the standard seats of a rabbinical synagogue are scanty, and oriental carpets cover the floor. The walls of the yard are decorated by inscriptions giving historical details.

Services held on Sabbaths and holidays are conducted by **Yosef Sadik,** the last Karaite *hazan* (cantor). Since no Karaite rabbi is available in Istanbul, members occasionally consult local Orthodox rabbis on religious matters.

The Karaite synagogue is part of a larger complex encircled by stone walls. The main entrance leads into a large courtyard, one side of which is lined with wooden houses. The current Muslim residents of these dilapidated houses relate that 50 years ago Karaite families inhabited these dwellings. They can even reel off several names such as those of Avram Yako and Ilya Marko.

Karaite Jews of Hasköy streamed to the newer neighborhoods of Galata and Şişli no less than did the Rabbinical Jews. The last remaining Karaite of Hasköy is a lovely old lady residing in the local Old Age Home. **Mary Yerushalmi's** fascinating life story is typical of many Karaites of her generation: Born and raised in the Crimean Peninsula, she settled in Hasköy with her family in the early years of the 20th century. The family later moved to Şişli, a more modern neighborhood of Istanbul. Yet the circle was completed when Mary took residence in the Old-Age Home of Hasköy some ten years ago, at her own request.

The equability reigning between Karaite and Rabbinical Jews of Hasköy during their lifetime is not violated at death. The local cemetery serves both congregations, a smaller plot being designated for the dwindling Karaite community.

The Jewish cemetery of Hasköy is situated on a hilltop north of the neighborhood. The construction of the Istanbul highway encircling the city caused great damage to the cemetery not too many years ago. Yet even prior to this intrusion, the cemetery had been badly neglected and overgrown by weeds.

The Hasköy cemetery is one of the largest Jewish cemeteries of Istanbul. The cemetery of Kuzguncuk had long been filled to capacity when this cemetery was opened in the late 19th century. It was probably the combined efforts of the Rabbinate and Karaite congregations that secured the building permit.

It is in this cemetery that the story of Abraham Camondo sounds its final note. Following his death, his body was returned to Istanbul for burial in the Hasköy cemetery. Here, in his magnificent stone tomb, the great philanthropist who did so much for Hasköy can continue to gaze at the beloved city from which he was exiled.

The **Old-Age Home of Hasköy** is the last stop on our tour. Known as *Moshav Zekinim* in Hebrew, it is known locally in Turkish as "İhtiyarlara Yardım Derneği". Initiated by the Ashkenazi leadership, the building formerly housed an AIU school and a rabbinical seminary prior to being converted to its present use some 20 years ago. The inscription of the original AIU facilities is still visible over the main entrance of this impressive and well-preserved building.

Some 80 elderly members of the community currently reside in the Home. Tended by professional medical workers in addition to volunteers from the community, these residents form the last bulwark against the ravages that time has wrought on the once flourishing Jewish community of Hasköy. For several of the residents the arc has swung full circle: the AIU building that once served as their educational center is now the haven of their remaining years. (The Old-Age Home is located in Köy Mektep Sokak, Tel: 2506988).

Beyoğlu District
Galata-Pera-Şişhane-Karaköy-Tünel

General Orientation: Centrally located though this area is, its unique topography allows for limited access to many of the following sites. These sites are by and large situated in the area between the Galata Bridge-Harbor and the Galata Tower-Tünel Sq.- İstiklal Caddesi-Taksim Sq.
The following routes lead to this vicinity: 1) The Tünel (subway) from its entrance (near the Galata Bridge) up to its stop on İstiklal Caddesi; (2) Yüksek Kaldırım Sokak up to İstiklal Caddesi (via Galip Dede Sokak); (3) İstiklal Caddesi is also accessible via the neighborhood of Şişhane, while passing along the Turkish Airlines office; (4) Those coming from the north could follow Cumhuriyet Caddesi via Taksim Sq. to İstiklal Caddesi.

The district described below is in fact divided into several neighborhoods. It was only in the mid-19th century that the entire area came under a single authority — the Beyoğlu District Municipality. Each neighborhood was officially well-defined, yet the confines of each neighborhood are not always clear even to people who have spent all their life in the area. Just to complicate the issue, some neighborhoods are known with more than one name. Thus, the old names of Pera and Galata have been newly designated Beyoğlu and Karaköy.

The main neighborhoods of this district containing Jewish sites are: **Galata/Karaköy** (including Şişhane) and **Beyoğlu/Pera** (including Tünel Sq., Tepebaşı, İstiklal Caddesi up to Taxim Sq.)

Most of the sites are located in the following streets:

(1) Büyük Hendek & Şair Ziya Paşa (Şişhane); (2) Yüksek Kaldırım & Alageyik (Karaköy); (3) Galip Dede - İstiklal Caddesi - Tünel Sq. (Beyoğlu). A good starting point for our tour would be the Galata Tower, from which most of these important routes emanate.

Major Jewish sites in this area: (1) 5 synagogues

(Zulfaris, Edirneli, Neve Şalom, Ashkenazi & Italian); (2) the chief rabbinate & community offices; (3) 3 schools; (4) Jewish commercial centers; and (5) Jewish residences.

The routes to these Jewish points of interest are paved with many fascinating sites of more general interest. So, for instance, the visitor will find several well-known buildings such as the Galatasaray Lycée, the Beyoğlu Municipality, the Galip Dede Museum, as well as a plethora of speciality shops and foreign consulates. Presiding over these colorful attractions looms the ancient Galata Tower, eternal symbol of this district.

General Historical Background

Twice in Ottoman history the district of Beyoğlu has played an extraordinary role in the drama of city life. The Ottoman conquest of Constantinople (1453) provided the background for its first rise to prominence when its Italian population assisted in the capture of the city.

The grateful conquerors rewarded the residents of this neighborhood with a generous measure of autonomy, as the inscription of the Galata Tower testifies. These privileges, along with a naturally favored strategic location, ensured the local merchants of continued success in the economic life of the Ottoman Empire. The residents of this district, many of whom were Jews, functioned as an important channel of communication for the various routes linking Istanbul to the outside world.

Once again, in the 19th century, this district rose to the forefront of national interest. Following the Tanzimat Reforms of 1839, Beyoğlu became the model of a westernized urban metropolis, the pattern for all dreams of modernization in the Levant. The hub of many foreigners as well as a large number of local non-Muslims, this area formed the unchallenged cultural and diplomatic heart of the Empire. No foreign embassy or major cultural and financial center was without representation in this district.

Educational centers as well as financial headquarters were situated there. These were the days when the **Grand Rue de Péra** (today's İstiklal Caddesi) and the opulent **Pera Palace Hotel** held sway over this vibrantly modern district.

Modern thoroughfares and convenient means of transport totally revamped the face of this district. Crumbling battlements were swept away in 1863, thus facilitating the plans for modernization. Thus did Büyük Hendek Caddesi, a crowded road in the heart of the Jewish neighborhood formerly divided by these walls, find itself metamorphosed into one of the first modern streets of Istanbul. It was even the first street to boast that outlandish new invention: gas-lit lamps. Brick houses rapidly replaced the old wooden ones, to the enormous relief of a population ever haunted by fear of fire.

Local transportation changed overnight with the completion of the city subway (Tünel) and the tramway which traversed İstiklal Caddesi. The 1875 completion of the Tünel was treated as a national celebration, and as a grand victory for the proponents of modernization.

The Tünel constituted an engineering feat by regional standards. 554.80 meters long, 6.70 meters wide and 4.90 meters high it did indeed contribute to the improvement of urban life. No longer did residents have to wrestle with the narrow and crowded Yüksek Kaldırım Sokak.

This district, and the neighborhoods of Pera and Galata in particular, evolved in the 19th century into the very financial core of the Empire. The numerous banks and well-equipped stores lining the major streets of this district reflected the supremacy of its status.

Many of these commercial centers were founded and managed by Jews in the late 19th and early 20th centuries. Over a dozen Jewish banks, connected with the Stock Exchange of Karaköy, were operating here by the end of the 19th century.

In the midst of all this thriving Jewish enterprise the figure of **Abraham Camondo** stands unique. By far the most important Jewish businessman of the city, he commanded a vast network of commercial and financial interests. A landlord of stupendous holdings, he held many buildings of Beyoğlu among his financial assets. Today, the names of many edifices preserve Camondo's heritage long after the family ownerwhip has lapsed: of them, the most famous are the "Camondo Steps" (Merdiven) located in **Voyvoda Sokak,** which formerly served as Camondo's financial headquarters. The stairs were restored in 1985 by the Beyoğlu Municipality, Demir Bank and the Austrian Gymnasium, as mentioned on a plaque situated there.

This district remains a prosperous business center for many Jews, although they no longer reside there as in former times.

But all was not high finance and business; communal and spiritual claims made demands of their own. The Italians and Ashkenazim established schools and synagogues. The neighborhood of Karaköy became a focus of Karaite life as Hasköy dwindled into relative insignificance.

The rapid pace of development was boosted by a large wave of Jewish refugees, Ashkenazim and Karaites from eastern Europe. Fleeing pogroms and political unrest, these new-comers introduced European ways and manners into the lifeblood of this district.

Cultural life flourished as it never had before. The well-known **Galatasaray Lycée** on İstiklal Caddesi, inaugurated in 1868, emerged as the symbol of educational modernization. Of the 341 students that year, 34 were Jewish. In an effort to encourage Jewish enrollment in state schools, authorities provided for the special religious needs of the Jewish students. Graduates of the modern state schools, amongst them many Jews, often became highly placed government officials.

Nevertheless, Jewish-sponsored schools, such as

the **Alliance Israélite Universelle** (AIU) remained the preferred educational option. Some of these educational facilities exist to this very day, such as the large deserted AIU building of Galata located in Dibek Sokak behind the Galata Tower. Nowadays, only two schools remain in a neighborhood that once boasted so many.

This district functions as the headquarters for many of the leading communal institutions, including: the chief rabbinate (23, Yemenici Sokak, Tünel); the community offices (61, Büyük Hendek Caddesi, Şişhane - next to Neve Şalom synagogue); the offices of the Italian and Ashkenazi congregations (adjacent to their synagogues).

The Italian synagogue of Karaköy

This area is deeply rooted in the collective consciousness of the community, for the many internal rifts, and even occasional eruptions, over matters both political and cultural reached their dramatic denouement on this stage.

In 1857, Beyoğlu was officially proclaimed "The Sixth District", a model for urban reform and local self-government. Thus did Beyoğlu become the first district to possess an independent municipality, administered by elected representatives. It was a sign of the times that both Muslims and non-Muslims served together in these assemblies. Abraham Camondo was an active member of this new municipality, initiating many of the modernizing reforms. (The Old Municipality building is located at the corner of Müellif and Yolcuzade İskender Sokak, in the vicinity of the Turkish Airlines Terminal.)

Whereas the modern district of Pera served as the economic center of the local Jews, Galata functioned as the spiritual and cultural center for all of Istanbul Jewry. The rapidly developing neighborhood of Pera acted as a magnet for many of the wealthier Jews of Galata. The environs of İstiklal Caddesi and Taksim Sq. became the residential and commercial hub of Jewish life in the new neighborhood. Prosperous though the neighborhood was, Pera proved to be but a passing stage for many Jews who eventually opted for the comforts of newer neighborhoods of the north, or emigration abroad.

Beyoğlu - Site by Site

Our tour will commence with a place more evocative than any other of Jewish Galata — the **Galata Tower** (Galata Kulesi). [The Tower was first built in 507 A.D. as a watch tower against fire and later restored in 1423. Height: 16.45 meters; radius: 3.75 meters. Open daily: 9:00-17:00. Elevator to the roof top — a fine observation point].

When a local Jewish theatre troop depicted the colorful flavor of local Jewish life on stage several years ago, no name was found more suitable for the play than "Kule" (Tower). Long the local symbol of Galata, it is the very geographical heart of this neighborhood. And for decades this area also constituted the core of Jewish life in Istanbul.

If it were not for the frequently elegant European dress of many of its residents, a visitor to this area on any Sabbath or holiday might have easily mistaken Galata for a typical eastern European *Shtetl*. Synagogues thronged the courtyards of this neighborhood. And to complete the picture, local banks were closed on Saturdays by order of the Sultan himself.

Many buildings were built and inhabited by Jews, as testified by the Hebrew dates embossed on the lintels above many a doorway. Observe closely the entrances to the apartment buildings at No 5 and 7, Tımarcı Sokak adjacent to Galata Tower. The Hebrew date 5652 corresponds to 1892, and 5654 yields 1893. For another example, observe the Star of David engraved on the facade of the home located just opposite the Neve Şalom synagogue in 50, Büyük Hendek Caddesi.

Many visitors will recognize the Spanish-style architecture of some local houses. Built around a central courtyard, a house of this type was popularly known as a "Jewish House" (Yahudi Hanı) since these houses had been constructed for and by Jews. Such a house might commonly be inhabited by members of an extended family, or members of a particular congregation or guild. In an era when change was rife and the modernization process often unsettling, this style of architecture helped the families to preserve the traditions and solidarity they had enjoyed in their former less-advanced neighborhoods.

A typical home of this kind is the 1893-built ornate and relatively well-preserved building located not far from Galata Tower in 56, Serdari Ekrem Sokak.

Many of the local apartment buildings were owned by Jewish landlords, chiefly the Camondo family. Such is the building known as the **Camondo Khan**, located in Küçük Hendek Caddesi, and the rather solid building located opposite the chief rabbinate in Yeminici Sokak.

Several major Jewish sites are located in Şişhane — a small neighborhood converging on Galata Tower. Şişhane's major road, Büyük Hendek Caddesi, is the very same one inaugurated as one of Istanbul's first modern thoroughfares.

The **Neve Şalom** synagogue, at No. 67, is surely the most famous Jewish site of this neighborhood. Although the present building was erected only in 1952, a synagogue bearing the same name had been standing here already in the 15th century. Neve Şalom (Oasis of Peace) is one of the largest and most active synagogues in the city. Containing nearly 500 seats, its interior is of a singularly impressive appearance. Although few local Jews regularly attend daily services, it is generally well-attended on holidays and special events.

The Neve Şalom synagogue became world famous due to the tragedy of September 6, 1986. On this Sabbath morning, 21 worshippers were massacred by terrorists. The terrorists burst through the entrance, killing the elderly *shamash* who had for decades tended the synagogue, and opened fire on the worshippers inside. The terrorists then fled through an adjacent alley.

The massacre shocked the Jewish community of Istanbul. It was deeply condemned by all Turkish circles, and many Turkish high-ranking officials attended the funerals and the memorial service. Most leading Turkish newspapers and periodicals carried in-depth reporting of the event, while concurrently informing the public of Turkish-Jewish history.

An annual memorial service is held on the site of the massacre. Following the service, the bereaved families lay a wreath of flowers on the graves of the victims in the Ashkenazi cemetery of Ulus.

Following the desecration of this holy building, regular religious services were suspended. It was only following the reconsecration one year later that the synagogue was reopened to the public, after a restoration made possible by donations that flowed in from World Jewry.

A commemorative plaque listing the names of the victims was placed inside the synagogue. Just underneath the plaque stands a tall grandfather clock. Local people relate that the clock stopped working when the shooting broke out at 9:17 that Sabbath morning. When the clock was later reinstated in the reconsecrated synagogue, the hands again began to move.

The tragedy sent a shockwave through the entire Jewish community. Sophisticated means are now used to protect all Jewish institutions of Istanbul. Entrance to the Neve Şalom synagogue requires special permit, obtainable at the adjoining office (tel: 2441576).

Up until some 20 years ago, another synagogue named "**Kneset Israel**" operated not far from the Neve Şalom synagogue (87, Büyük Hendek Caddesi). The synagogue, erected in 1923, was later turned into a sports club (Yıldırım Spor Klübü, Tel: 2493415).

Just down the street are **two Jewish schools:** "Musevi I. Karma İlkokulu" an elementary school, established some 75 years ago, and a high school, "Beyoğlu Özel Musevi Lisesi", founded by B'nai Brith in 1915.

Not far from these schools, in Dibek Sokak stands the abandoned old Alliance Israélite Universelle school, established in 1912 with the assistance of the Camondo family. After its closure in the middle of the present century, the building served for a few years as an orphanage, replacing a similar institution located in Ortaköy.

The **Italian synagogue** is also located in Şişhane, not far from the Neve Şalom synagogue (27, Şair Ziya Paşa Yokuşu Sokak Tel: 2447784). This synagogue, recently renovated, was founded in 1887 to serve the small yet vibrant local Italian congregation (approximately 500 persons). Italian Jews had lived in this area under the Byzantines, and a steady stream continued to arrive throughout the Ottoman era.

A dispute over the question of marriage in the mid-19th century erupted into a major rift between the central Jewish leadership and Daniel Farandis, head of the Italian congregation. The ensuing tension resulted in the formation of a separate Italian synagogue. The new congregation was composed not only of Italian Jews, but also those Jews of Bulgarian descent who found themselves dissatisfied with the traditional Jewish hierarchy.

The Italian-Jewish congregation of Galata maintained close relations with the Italian Embassy of Istanbul. By request of the Italian government, Sultan Abdülaziz in 1866 granted the Italian Jews a plot in Galata on which to build their synagogue. The synagogue functioned for nearly 30 years prior to its official inauguration. The charming fountain of the courtyard bears the inscription "The Holy Italian Congregation 1866".

The congregation has maintained a steady membership of some 500 worshippers, most of whom reside in the Şişli district. Daily services are conducted regularly, even though the presiding rabbi is no longer Italian. Administrative affairs are managed by an elected council supervised by the chief rabbinate. (Office of the Italian Congregation: 17, Küçük Hendek Sokak)

In this same area between the Italian synagogue and Büyük Hendek Caddesi, the *Matzot* factory for unleavened bread is located, supplying the Passover needs of the local community.

South of the area between Galata Tower and Galata Bridge, two synagogues are situated, both of them closed due to their regretable state of deterioration.

1) **Edirneli synagogue:** 1, Felek Sokak, named after the city of Edirne, home town to many immigrant Jews in Istanbul in the late Ottoman period. The synagogue originally served the

Ashkenazi congregation, whose offices stand on the other side of the same building.

2) **Zolfaris synagogue** — located in the narrow Perçemli Sokak not far from the Tünel entrance near the Galata Bridge. Existing since the second half of the 17th century, the synagogue was subsequently restored in 1890 with a donation from the Camondo family. Closed to the public for nearly 10 years, its interior is in an advanced state of decay. Thieves have only aggravated the damage wrought by time. But it would seem that a new era is in store for this synagogue. A top priority for the Committee of the 500th anniversary celebrations, plans for extensive renovation are underway. Ultimately, the building will be outfitted as a Jewish museum. (For entrance inquire in the chief rabbinate).

Yüksek Kaldırım Sokak — the only street linking lower and upper Galata — has an impressive Jewish history as well. Along with the adjoining Voyvoda and Bankalar Sokak, it has long served as one of the major financial and residential centers of the local Jewish community.

For the visitor interested in Jewish heritage, the **Ashkenazi synagogue** would be the most important site in this street (at No. 37). Its inauguration ceremony was presided over by the Austrian ambassador, Baron De Calice. The façade of the building bears the inscripion "Germano-Israélite".

One of the most beautiful and well-preserved synagogues of Istanbul, it serves the needs of some 1000 Ashkenazi members. The lavish weddings celebrated in this edifice are renowned throughout Istanbul. Sephardic rabbis have for the past 50 years or so presided over a congregation that no longer boasts an Ashkenazi rabbi. Administered by an elected council, the assembly is subordinate to the chief rabbinate. (office address: 10, Banker Sokak, Tel: 1442975).

Just behind the Ashkenazi synagogue in Alageyik Sokak we come across the ruins of another synagogue gutted by fire some 50 years ago. Decayed though it is, traces of its past magnificence linger on.

The gate of the courtyard bears the following Hebrew inscription: "How goodly are thy tents O Ya'akov, and thy tabernacles O Israel." Just above this inscription are engraved the Ten Commandments.

Through the debris one can still view the lovely spiral staircase that leads to the women's section, and the niche of the Holy Ark. Intriguing though the synagogue is, entrance is nevertheless not recommended due to its hazardous condition.

During the 19th century the Ashkenazi congregation administered the neighborhood school. In its day the Ashkenazi Boys School, run by the renowned Mr. Goldshmidt, was something of a local landmark. The language of instruction was German.

The final major point of attraction is the **building of the chief rabbinate** [23, Yemenici Sokak, Beyoğlu/Tünel (near the Tünel Sq.) Tel: 2448794/5]. The large, 5-storey building was built in the early 20th century. It was here, in the very same building, that a recognized central chief rabbinate was organized for the first time. This building also serves as the headquarters of the community council, thus functioning as the major spiritual and political center of Turkish Jewry. The unprepossessing façade gives way to a far more ornate interior. Handsome frescoes embellish the ceiling, and antique objets d'art are strewn about the lofty rooms.

The office of the chief rabbi is located in the most spacious room of the building. Other rooms are utilized by members of the court, or serve as library and secretariat. Portraits of famous rabbis and representations of historical events line the walls. One picture features the assembly of Turkish-Jewish leaders held in this very building some 20 years ago.

Facing the chief rabbinate stands a large and rather dingy building. Now abandoned, it once housed the headquarters of the magnate Abraham Camondo. This edifice is one of the many buildings that once sheltered Jewish residents and merchants of the neighborhood. Nowadays Jews no longer reside in this neighborhood, even though they might frequent social clubs in the area.

Strolling down Meşrutiyet Caddesi (named after the constitutional period of the Ottoman Empire), one can glimpse the impressive Beyoğlu palace, home of the **first local Municipality**. The palace, erected in the 19th century in the flush of contemporary reforms, became the landmark of the district. It was in this building that local residents enjoyed a form of self-government for the first time in Ottoman history.

Contemporary records indicate that Jewish residents of the district received ample representation in these assemblies. Thus did that ever-present figure of Abraham Camondo find himself one of the 5 dignitaries who supervised the nuts and bolts of urban political reform. Another Jew, the merchant **Reuben**, was elected to the district council in 1878.

On the other side of Meşrutiyet Caddesi (bordering the American consulate general) we see another well-known building of prime importance to local Jewish history: The legendary **Pera Palace Hotel.** This impressive hotel, established in 1892 for the sole enjoyment of passengers of the Orient Express, became the residence of wealthy Russian Jews who had fled upheavals in their native country. Several Zionist leaders, during their stay in Istanbul, made this hotel their headquarters. Countless international spies (or so it is rumored) passed through the elegant lobby of this grand hotel. Operations for the rescue of European Jewry, — Hungarian Jewry in particular, were frequently negotiated here during the Second World War.

Tepebaşı, located next to the Pera Palace Hotel, is one of Istanbul's finest observation points. The entire expanse of the Golden Horn, with the neighborhoods of Balat and Hasköy spilling over either shore, can be easily watched from this fine vantage point. The routes of Jewish migration throughout Istanbul are better comprehended from this panoramic view. The dilapidated homes of the old neighborhoods appear shabbier than ever when compared with the handsome stone buildings of the more modern neighborhoods.

Looking from Tepebaşı down to Kasımpaşa, one can clearly see an **ornamented palace** situated on the northern bank of the Golden Horn. It is believed that this building, currently occupied by the Turkish Navy headquarters, formerly served as the private residence of Abraham Camondo.

From Tepebaşı, the lovely Flower Market and Pera Passage lead us back to the heart of İstiklal Caddesi. Here we find the previously mentioned **Galatasaray Lycée,** the first modern school of Istanbul. Continuing down İstiklal Caddesi up to Taksim Sq. we come across our final tour site for today.

Taxim Square was a center of Jewish life up until some 50 years ago. The name of the square indicates its former designation as a center for water distribution. The magnificent monument dominating the square was built by an Italian architect in 1928 to celebrate the Turkish Republic. On the other side of the square we find the Atatürk Cultural Center. The luxuriant, green lawns of Taksim Park are relatively new; the same area once served as a non-Muslim cemetery. Upon creation of the park in the 19th century, the graves were reinterred in the cemeteries of Şişli.

The Modern Districts of the European Shore:
Şişli-Osmanbey-Nişantaş-Teşvikiye-Ulus

The district of Şişli has undergone a rapid development during the course of the present century, particularly over the past 50 years. Gradually, it has replaced Beyoğlu as the leading modern district of Istanbul.

Vast numbers of people resettled in this district, and Jews did not lag behind. Within a relatively short period of time, Şişli became the hub of Jewish life for all Istanbul. Residing now in Şişli, many Jews continued to conduct their business in Beyoğlu.

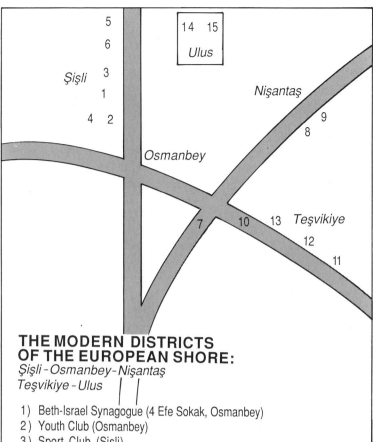

THE MODERN DISTRICTS
OF THE EUROPEAN SHORE:
Şişli - Osmanbey - Nişantaş
Teşvikiye - Ulus

1) Beth-Israel Synagogue (4 Efe Sokak, Osmanbey)
2) Youth Club (Osmanbey)
3) Sport Club (Şişli)
4) Cultural Club
5) Jewish-Italian-Cemetery (Abide-i Hürriyet Caddesi, Şişli)
6) Christian Cemeteries
7) Vali Konağı Caddesi (Israeli Consulate, Nişantaş)
8) Şalom Newspaper (Kuyulu Bostan Sokak, Nişantaş)
9) American Hospital (Nişantaş)
10) Teşvikiye Caddesi
11) Teşvikiye (Sabbatian/Dönme) Mosque (150 Teşvikiye Caddesi)
12) Şişli Terakki Sabbatian school (162 Teşvikiye Caddesi)
13) Işık Sabbatian school (151 Teşvikiye Caddesi)
14) Ashkenazi Cemetery (Memorial for the victims of the Neve-Şalom massacre; at Zincirlikuyu Caddesi, Ulus)
15) Sephardi (Arnavuktöy) Cemetery (Zincirlikuyu Caddesi, Ulus)

The quarter's synagogue is **Beth-Israel,** located in 4, Efe Sokak, in Osmanbey, near the intersection of Rumeli and Halaskargazi Caddesi (tel: 2406599). The relatively new synagogue (b. 1981) is one of the most active in Istanbul. Graced by the chief rabbi and many other dignitaries, its walls hum with the sound of the many worshippers who gather there on Saturdays and holidays.

A Passover *Seder* is conducted there by the chief rabbi himself. Over 500 seats, and a special women's section, accommodate the many worshippers. As in Jewish communities the world over, an active Sunday school and youth club provide religious education for the younger members of the community. Like all Jewish institutions in Turkey, this synagogue too is well-protected by sophisticated means. Entrance is accessible only by pre-arrangement.

Most **major clubs of the community** are located in the vicinity of the synagogue: The Youth Club (Kültür ve Sanat Yurdu Derneği, or "*Amikal*" — as it is widely known), established in 1910, is the largest Jewish youth club of Turkey, and a very active one indeed. Weekly programs offer a wide variety of educational and cultural activities. Young Jewish university students in particular flock to this pleasant meeting place (Tel: 2406599).

The Jewish Sports Club of Istanbul, "Yıldırım" (Star), is also located in this neighborhood; the basketball team plays regularly in the city league (Tel: 2403870).

But the club most generally frequented by one and all is the 1966-formed Friendship Club (Arkadaşlık Yurdu Derneği). Particularly popular amongst elder members of the community, its large performance hall often hosts various shows and concerts (Tel: 2483336).

Another Jewish site in Şişli, of quite a different order, is the **Italian-Jewish cemetery** (located on Abide-i Hürriyet Caddesi, not far from Şişli mosque). This cemetery, and the adjoining Catholic and Armenian ones, were transferred here from Taksim

Park in the 19th century. Once a wide and open space, the cemeteries now find themselves in the midst of a crowded urban area.

Of these three cemeteries the Jewish one is the smallest. Its gate faces Abide-i Hürriyet Caddesi and is generally closed to visitors. The well-preserved cemetery was built in 1866. The story behind its establishment is unfolded on the imposing gates in both Hebrew and Italian: "Thanks to the representation of the Italian government, Sultan Abdülaziz graciously granted this burial plot in 1866 to the residing Jewish community, under the auspices of the Italian government".

Thus do we have another example of the privileges enjoyed by those Ottoman Jews possessing foreign citizenship. Though nowadays still in service, the cemetery is no longer used strictly by members of the Italian congregation.

The adjacent neighborhood of Nişantaş boasts a particularly large and well-to-do Jewish community, which settled there in the mid-20th century. Nişantaş' main street, Vali Konağı Caddesi, has been particularly favored by many local Jews. A number of stores and trading centers in this street and its surroundings are run by Jews. The **Israeli consulate general** is located on this street as well (no. 73/4). The leading hospital of the city — the **American Hospital** — is also situated in this area.

The publishers of the **Jewish weekly** Şalom are located in this neighborhood [Kuyucu Bostan Sokak, Mola Apartmant, 2/3]. Şalom, presently the only Jewish newspaper of Turkey, was established in 1940 by Abraham Leon. Upon the demise of its founder in 1985, the newspaper passed into the hands of the Jewish-owned company, "Gözlem Gazetecilik".

The newspaper layout adheres to the special language requirements of its readers; seven pages are written in Turkish, and the remaining page in Ladino (Judeo-İspanyol). The weekly's editor-in-chief is Silvio Ovadia; and the general editor of the Ladino section is Salamon Bicirano. All staff members work on a voluntary basis. *Şalom* has a circulation of some 3,000 readers, many of whom live outside Turkey. Unique paper that it is, its regular subscribers include many libraries and research centers around the world.

The neighborhood of Teşvikiye, located between Nişantaş and Macka, contains perhaps the most curious religious group ever to evolve from Judaism. This has been the major center of the **Sabbatian community** ever since they first immigrated to Istanbul from Saloniki in the early 20th century.

The Sabbatians, locally known as Dönme or Selanikliler, transferred to Teşvikiye not only their families and skills but also their well-developed communal institutions. Thus, they have succeeded in preserving their age-old traditions, customs and family ties in their new homeland. Of the many population groups forced to emigrate following the upheavals of the early 20th century, the Sabbatians have certainly proved to be the most stable.

The Sabbatian mosque of Saloniki, built in 1902, served the local congregation for only a brief period of time. Upon arriving in Istanbul, members of this sect established a mosque of their own in this neighborhood of Teşvikiye, and it has functioned ever since as their major spiritual center (the mosque is located at 150, Teşvikiye Caddesi). Whether or not the Sabbatians still maintain vestiges of Orthodox Jewry in another building entirely separate from the Muslim mosque, is a matter of some controversy.

Although the total area of the Teşvikiye mosque is large, its interior is relatively small. A highly ornate building, its curving walls are hung with handsome oriental carpets. The mosque is open to visitors (except at times of prayer). A well-tended garden encircles the mosque. Monumental pillars are engraved with ornamental inscriptions in Ottoman style. Funeral ceremonies are occasionally conducted in this mosque. Once the ceremonial rituals have been completed, the mourners usually continue to the Sabbatian cemetery in the Asian neighborhood of Üsküdar (see Üsküdar).

Adjacent to the Teşvikiye mosque are **two schools** established by Sabbatian immigrants from Saloniki. The Şişli Terakki (162, Teşvikiye Caddesi), and the Işık (15 Teşvikiye Caddesi) are schools that have an enrollment of many Sabbatian as well as Jewish children. First established in Saloniki respectively in 1885 and 1879, the dates inscribed upon the school gates commemorate the year of their transfer to Istanbul. The existence of two separate schools reflects the split that characterizes the Sabbatian sect. Each school is supervised by the leadership of one of the two major divisions: Kapancılar (Terraki) and Karakaşlar (Işık).

Several other institutions such as clinics are maintained by Sabbatians and cater for the needs of their local co-religionists.

As is often the case, the prestige of the Şişli-Nişantaş district has dimmed in recent years, while at the same time witnessing a loss of its residents as many Jews moved to newer neighborhoods. One of the most sought-after destinations is the more luxurious district of Etiler-Levent-Ulus. The Jewish community of this area is growing apace, even though neither synagogues nor Jewish clubs have thus far been established.

The **two Jewish cemeteries** located side by side in Ulus (in Zincirlikuyu Caddesi, near the Bulgarian consulate) were established prior to this influx. One cemetery is named Arnavutköy Musevi Mezarlığı (tel: 2643359). The Ashkenazi Cemetery, though so named, no longer serves a strictly Ashkenazi congregation. (Aşkenaz Musevi Mezarlığı; tel: 2701380). It is in this cemetery that the victims of the Neve Şalom massacre were laid to rest. (Both cemeteries are surrounded by high walls and controlled by guards; visitors have access everyday except Saturdays and Jewish holidays).

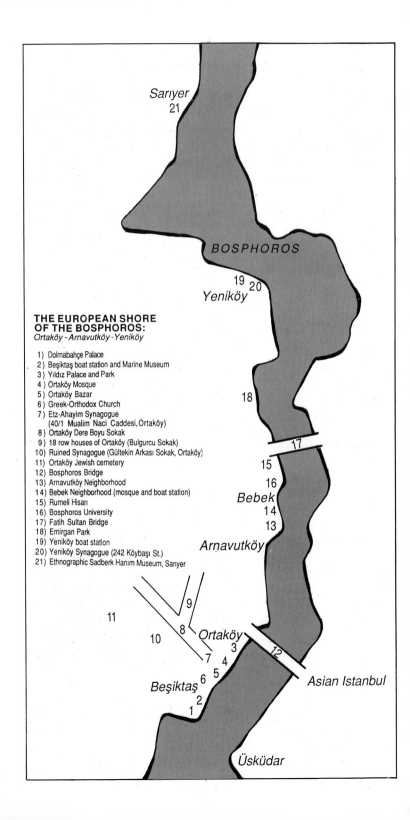

Sarıyer
21

BOSPHOROS

19 20
Yeniköy

**THE EUROPEAN SHORE
OF THE BOSPHOROS:**
Ortaköy - Arnavutköy - Yeniköy

1) Dolmabahçe Palace
2) Beşiktaş boat station and Marine Museum
3) Yıldız Palace and Park
4) Ortaköy Mosque
5) Ortaköy Bazar
6) Greek-Orthodox Church
7) Etz-Ahayim Synagogue
   (40/1 Mualim Naci Caddesi, Ortaköy)
8) Ortaköy Dere Boyu Sokak
9) 18 row houses of Ortaköy (Bulgurcu Sokak)
10) Ruined Synagogue (Gültekin Arkası Sokak, Ortaköy)
11) Ortaköy Jewish cemetery
12) Bosphoros Bridge
13) Arnavutköy Neighborhood
14) Bebek Neighborhood (mosque and boat station)
15) Rumeli Hisarı
16) Bosphoros University
17) Fatih Sultan Bridge
18) Emirgan Park
19) Yeniköy boat station
20) Yeniköy Synagogue (242 Köybaşı St.)
21) Ethnographic Sadberk Hanım Museum, Sarıyer

18

17

15
16
Bebek
14
13

Arnavutköy

9
11
8
10   *Ortaköy*
7   3
     4   12
  6 5
Beşiktaş
     2   *Asian Istanbul*
  1

Üsküdar

The European Shore of the Bosphorus
Ortaköy-Arnavutköy-Yeniköy

Ancient and colorful, the neighborhoods located along the European shore of the Bosphorus, between Beşiktaş and Büyükdere, have sheltered a small but thriving Jewish community ever since the early days of the Ottoman conquest. A map dating from the 17th century indicates that Jews and Muslims constituted the two single largest groups in Beşiktaş. Jews formed the largest ethno-religious group in both Ortaköy and Kuruçeşme, whereas in the neighborhood of Arnavutköy the largest communities were those of the Greeks and the Jews. By the late 19th century some 3000 Jews were to be found in Beşiktaş, and approximately three hundred in the neighborhoods of Arnavutköy and Büyükdere.

The fires that swept so devastatingly through these areas in the 18th and 19th centuries prompted many Jews to seek improved living conditions in the modern neighborhoods of Galata and Şişli. Fire was a major cause of a neighborhood's decay, often reducing formerly wealthy Jews to rags overnight. The destruction of six synagogues by fire in 1813 could only have demoralized an already crumbling community.

Of all these Jewish neighborhoods, Ortaköy was to retain the most dominant Jewish presence. Jews settled there in so steady a stream that by 1903 the 637 families of the 17th century had swelled to nearly 7000 people. Even the attractions of the newer modern neighborhoods could not dim Ortaköy's appeal, and it remained a major Jewish center up through the mid-20th century. It was only due to the mass emigration to the State of Israel after 1948 that Ortaköy reverted to its role of an aging grande dame whose days of glory had faded. Today only some twenty or thirty elderly Jews remain who can speak firsthand of life in this once so colorful quarter.

Only **one active synagogue** survives in the neighborhood (a second one, located in Gültekin Arkası Sokak, has been out of use for some 30 years), and it is here in the Etz-Ahayim synagogue that one can find the community center and offices. The synagogue is located on the main waterfront road not far from the Ortaköy mosque at 40/1 Muallim Naci Caddesi (tel: 2601896). From the handsome façade and well-preserved appearance, one would never guess that this is one of the city's oldest synagogues. The ravages of fire have been tempered by the benefits of renovation; the last major restorations were carried out in 1913, as inscribed above the entrance gate, and then again in 1941, following a fire which left the interior of the synagogue almost completely destroyed.

Lovely old objects culled from a variety of other synagogues are faithfully preserved here. Amongst these objects is an intricately chiselled stone gate bearing a dedication to the philanthropist Abraham Camondo; a gate that looks rather lost away from its original setting of a Holy Ark destroyed in the fire of 1941.

Etz-Ahayim synagogue in Ortaköy

Of a somewhat plain but still pleasing interior, a special women's gallery is located at the back. The few worshippers who gather for the daily prayers congregate in the small *Beit-Midrash* off the courtyard. Formerly, the *Beit-Midrash* was maintained by a local Ashkenazi congregation which settled in Ortaköy in the 19th century. Saturdays and festivals draw a considerably larger crowd; an outdoor brunch is always served after Sabbath morning prayers. Communal records are located in the small office; pictures illustrating various moments in the life of the community line the walls.

The Ortaköy synagogue is located in a particularly delightful area, one that has become a major center for art and entertainment. Cosy restaurants and tea houses abound, as do art galleries featuring the works of talented local artists. The outdoor art bazaar near the mosque, held every Sunday during the summer, makes this day the one most recommended for a pleasant excursion.

Pupils of a Jewish school in Ortaköy in the 1930's

The beautiful **mosque of Ortaköy** and the nearby Bosphorus Bridge offer a magnificent panorama, and the old and handsome Greek-Orthodox church is another visual treat. Yet beautiful though they are separately, they are even more special when viewed together. The existence of synagogue, church, and mosque side by side imbues the area with that special atmosphere characteristic of the old neighborhoods of Istanbul.

The main street of Ortaköy and the surrounding roads were formerly inhabited by numerous Jewish families. Old-timers can still point out certain buildings once occupied by Jews. One such house, the large wooden home at 52 Ortaköy Dere Boyu Caddesi, belonged to Jews prior to their emigration to Israel some forty years ago.

But of all these sights, surely none could be more evocative of Ortaköy than the **eighteen row houses** which line Bulgurcu Sokak in proud duplication. It is not by chance that eighteen such houses were constructed: Jews have long considered 18 a particularly propitious number, the very symbol of life itself. The wooden first story supporting two upper stories of stone is a particularly Jewish feature of the local architecture. Renovated several times since their construction in the 19th century, these houses nevertheless present a somewhat dilapidated appearance.

Formerly the neighborhood of Ortaköy housed several institutions serving the entire Jewish community of Istanbul. Such was the **local orphanage** operating there up until the mid-1970's. Several local schools established in the 19th century served the Jewish children of Ortaköy and its surroundings

The Ortaköy **Jewish cemetery** is situated on a hilltop near Çevirmeci Sokak. Though established only in the 19th century and enclosed by protective walls, the cemetery is nevertheless desolate and ill-kept. Of the tombstones that still remain many are left chipped and broken, scattered amongst the straggly patches of grass. This cemetery is only a fragment of its former size; many of the nearby apartment buildings are built on land appropriated from the cemetery grounds. The cemetery is easily visible from the Bosphorus Bridge.

Continuing north along the Bosphorus, one sees many fine old wooden villas along the shore. Some of these *yalı* are the former homes of affluent Jews, distinguished leaders of the Jewish community. So lovely were these homes, so eminent the residents, that the famous 17th-century traveller Evliya Çelebi did not fail to take special note of this area.

Local tradition assigns this location to the mansion of that most exalted of Jewish dignitaries, **Don Joseph Nasi** (1524-1579). The scion of the Mendes family of bankers, whose financial holdings embraced the world, the wealth and influence of Don Joseph was exceeded only by that of his aunt, the Dona Gracia. Refugees of the Portugese Inquisition, the family found a welcoming haven in the Serene Portal of the Ottoman Sultan, who appointed Don Joseph "Duke of Naxos". Well-established in government circles, neither Don Joseph nor his aunt ever failed to recognize the bond of destiny shared by all Jews. Events such as the Ancona Boycott, and an envisioned Jewish resettlement of Tiberias in the Holy Land, are events that have secured these two figures a firm place in Jewish history.

The nearby neighborhood of Arnavutköy ("Albanian Village") was also densely settled by Jews, many of whom resided in elegant waterside villas. The **Arnavutköy Jewish cemetery** is located on a hilltop in the modern neighborhood of Ulus. Of the many synagogues of this area, only the neighborhood of **Yeniköy** still retains its synagogue. It is located on the main road, next to the Yeniköy boat station (242 Köybaşı Caddesi).

It is with this lone surviving synagogue that the local Jewish heritage casts its lengthening shadows, but the area offers a rich profusion of sights of a more general nature: Yıldız and Emirgan Parks, Dolmabahçe Palace, Rumeli Hisarı, Bebek Mosque, the Bosphoros University and the American Robert College as well as Sariyer's ethnographic Sadberk Hanım Museum.

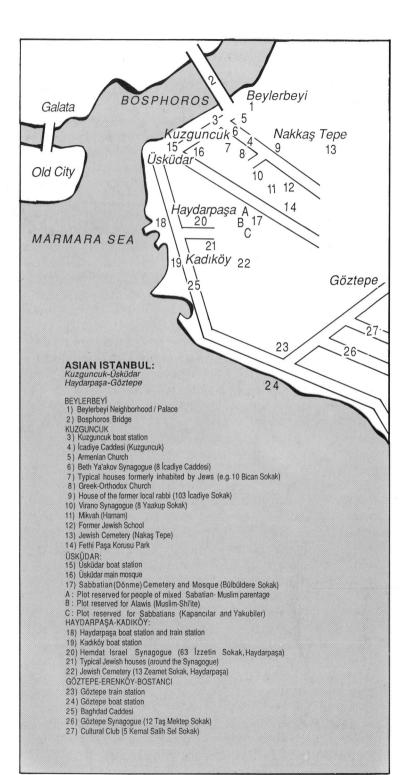

ASIAN ISTANBUL:
Kuzguncuk-Üsküdar
Haydarpaşa-Göztepe

BEYLERBEYİ
1) Beylerbeyi Neighborhood / Palace
2) Bosphoros Bridge
KUZGUNCUK
3) Kuzguncuk boat station
4) İcadiye Caddesi (Kuzguncuk)
5) Armenian Church
6) Beth Ya'akov Synagogue (8 İcadiye Caddesi)
7) Typical houses formerly inhabited by Jews (e.g.10 Bican Sokak)
8) Greek-Orthodox Church
9) House of the former local rabbi (103 İcadiye Sokak)
10) Virano Synagogue (8 Yaakup Sokak)
11) Mikvah (Hamam)
12) Former Jewish School
13) Jewish Cemetery (Nakaş Tepe)
14) Fethi Paşa Korusu Park
ÜSKÜDAR:
15) Üsküdar boat station
16) Üsküdar main mosque
17) Sabbatian(Dönme) Cemetery and Mosque (Bülbüldere Sokak)
A : Plot reserved for people of mixed Sabatian- Muslim parentage
B : Plot reserved for Alawis (Muslim-Shi'ite)
C : Plot reserved for Sabbatians (Kapancılar and Yakubiler)
HAYDARPAŞA-KADIKÖY:
18) Haydarpaşa boat station and train station
19) Kadıköy boat station
20) Hemdat İsrael Synagogue (63 İzzetin Sokak, Haydarpaşa)
21) Typical Jewish houses (around the Synagogue)
22) Jewish Cemetery (13 Zeamet Sokak, Haydarpaşa)
GÖZTEPE-ERENKÖY-BOSTANCI
23) Göztepe train station
24) Göztepe boat station
25) Baghdad Caddesi
26) Göztepe Synagogue (12 Taş Mektep Sokak)
27) Cultural Club (5 Kemal Salih Sel Sokak)

The Asian Shore of the Bosphorus:
Kuzguncuk-Üsküdar-Haydarpaşa-Göztepe

Although European Istanbul has ever been the prime attraction for Jewish settlement, the Asian side of Istanbul has been far from neglected. Indeed, Jews had founded thriving communities in the very first years of Ottoman rule, and during the 17th century their numbers were augmented by refugees of the fires that devastated so many neighborhoods on the European side of the city.

Of the three major Jewish centers flourishing by the 17th century, a contemporary map locates the most important center of all in Kuzguncuk; two smaller communities were found in Üsküdar and Çengelköy (near Beylerbeyi). By the late Ottoman period these centers had dwindled significantly as more and more Jews moved to modernized European districts or, after 1948, to the newly-declared State of Israel. The most recent years have brought something of a comeback for Asian Istanbul as numerous Jews came to live in the modern district of Göztepe. All in all, some 40% of Istanbul Jewry currently resides on the Asian shores of the city.

Kuzguncuk

Kuzguncuk is by far the most handsome of the many beautiful neighborhoods in Asian Istanbul, as well as the one most steeped in Jewish history. *Kuzguncuk can be reached by a variety of ways: (1) the Bosphorus bridge, turning right towards Üsküdar; (2) a direct boat line operating several times daily connects Kuzguncuk with Eminönü (Boğaz Hattı) via Beşiktaş; (3) alternatively, one could take the boat from either Eminönü (Üsküdar Station) or from Beşiktaş to Üsküdar, covering the remaining distance to Kuzguncuk by bus, dolmuş, or simply a pleasant 20-minute walk.*

An old and established village by the first years of Ottoman rule, Kuzguncuk was named in honor of a holy figure of local renown. Even in the midst of all the urban centers that have mushroomed close by,

Kuzguncuk has stubbornly managed to preserve its unique atmosphere and proud village spirit. A cultural center throughout the centuries, Kuzguncuk has been the home of many an artisan. Sumptuous villas, several of which were inhabited by Jews clustered together on the shores of the neighborhood. The later Ottoman period however witnessed a steady decline of the neighborhood, and decay and neglect set in. But most recently, Kuzguncuk has been undergoing something of a revival as more and more people with imagination and a love of old places have moved into the neighborhood, attracted by its lovely wooden houses and beautiful vistas.

İcadiye Caddesi is the one long street of Kuzguncuk, and is indeed the very heart and soul of this tiny neighborhood. The quaint wooden houses are mostly situated along this street and in its narrow, sunlit alleys. The restaurants along the water, the luxuriant foliage of ancient trees, the character and charm of the wooden houses all endow Kuzguncuk with a unique atmosphere. Proud of their neighborhood, residents are generally happy to regale the visitor with local anecdotes. The lane bearing the name Perihan Abla is one familiar to all Turks; a popular television series filmed on location bears this name. Photographs of its actors line the walls of the Kuzguncuk Community Center: the neighborhood barber shop.

Jews, Greek-Orthodox, and Armenians formed the major part of the neighborhood's population for over 400 years; the mosques dotting the streets here and there are a recent addition. Three impressive churches bear witness to a strong local Christian element that is no longer present.

For centuries, Jews constituted the dominant element of Kuzguncuk, numbering at its peak nearly 10,000 souls. The Jews who have moved on to other neighborhoods still retain a great affection for the neighborhood of their youth. Popularly known as "little Jerusalem", it was home to many rabbis and scholars. Some of the first modern Jewish schools had their beginnings here.

The Virano synagogue in Kuzguncuk

A Jewish house in Kuzguncuk

Nowadays, however, scarcely more than a dozen Jews still reside in Kuzguncuk, most of them elderly people who have clung tenaciously to the neighborhood of their birth. Like other local residents, these Jews too are of lesser means. But the arrival of Sabbath and festivals finds many additional Jews who have come to attend services in the old neighborhood. That community services still exist in the present reduced circumstances is due to the energy and efforts of one man, Mr. **Nissim Al-Bala,** the charming community president. Though no longer a resident of Kuzguncuk and busy as he is with his responsibility as administrator of the Or-Ahayim Hospital, Mr. Al-Bala still knows by name every single member of the community.

Jewish symbols such as *Mezuzas* and Stars of David are still etched on some of the fine old homes. The recent spate of local renovations has brushed the dust off many Hebrew dates. One home-owner, proud of the lineage of his home, has affixed the date of the house's foundation in Hebrew (5683), Latin (1923) and the Ottoman script (10 Bican Efendi Sokak).

Of special beauty are the houses on the corner of İcadiye Caddesi and Simitci Sokak. One of the Jewish families residing here was the **Bahar family**, who emigrated to Israel some 35 years ago. The house, located at İcadiye, no. 103 was the home of the last local rabbi. Kuzguncuk is a living example of the architectural style maintained by the Jews. Here can be found in great profusion the stone or red-brick foundations, topped by wooden upper stories so characteristic of Jewish homes all over Istanbul.

The **Beth Ya'akov synagogue** is the central synagogue of Kuzguncuk (8, İcadiye Caddesi tel: 3431699). Built in 1878, it serves the community during the summer months. The impressive interior is beautifully appointed, and together with the women's gallery on the second floor can seat some 250 worshippers. Old and rare scrolls are preserved in the Holy Ark; a lovely courtyard features a *Beit-Midrash.* It is interesting to note that a Greek-Orthodox church — small and no longer in use — is located just next door to the synagogue, and that an Armenian church and a mosque sit side by side just across the shore road.

The **Virano synagogue,** built in 1856, serves the community during the winter months (just off İcadiye Caddesi at 8, Yakup Sokak) The large two-story building, enclosed by high walls, is very impressive. The entrance gate is inscribed with the Hebrew founding date and the history of the synagogue; on the wall nearby a large Star of David is embossed. The second floor women's gallery is no longer in use, and women worshippers are seated at the back of the main hall.

Next to this winter synagogue is an old *hamam* which formerly served as a ritual bath (*mikvah*) for the Jewish community. The public school not far away (towards the upper part of the neighborhood) formerly functioned as the local Alliance Israélite Universelle school, and was built in the late 19th century.

Kuzguncuk cemetery, located rather far from the center, is one of the oldest in Istanbul. The Asian continent being considered sacred — perhaps for its proximity to the Land of Israel — the cemetery served Jews from all over Istanbul. Gravestones are ancient, and often beautifully inscribed with Biblical verses and Jewish symbols. These gravestones, and indeed their very choice of script, contain the tale of an entire Jewish community. Some of them perpetuate the memory of Jewish refugees from the Spanish Inquisition of the 16th century. Others tell the life story of Jews throughout the centuries. Hebrew and Ladino commemorate the earlier Jews; Ottoman-Arabic those who lived in much later times during the late 19th century, and the Latin characters of modern Turkish those recently deceased. A small plot is still, though infrequently, used.

Located at the top of a hill, Nakaş Tepe, the cemetery is surrounded by walls. Poorly preserved, many of the gravestones were used as local building material prior to the erection of the cemetery's walls. The cemetery is open to visitors every day but Saturday. The observation post at **Fethi Paşa Korusu** commands a perfect view of the cemetery.

Üsküdar

The neighborhood of Üsküdar can be reached from Kuzguncuk either via Bağlarbaşı (near the Jewish cemetery), or via the shore road. Regular boat lines connect Üsküdar with Eminönü, Kabataş and Beşiktaş.

One of the more intriguing neighborhoods of Istanbul, Üsküdar (old Skutari) is the most ancient of all on the Asian shores of the city. Engravings from the early Ottoman period depict a small rural village; the Üsküdar of today is a bustling and hardworking center of commerce. This neighborhood has been the traditional bastion of Islam; beautiful mosques and *hans* abound, many of them quite ancient. The ones located on Hakimiyet Milliye Caddesi, built by the famous architect Sinan, one just across from the other and recently renovated, are particularly noteworthy.

Predominantly Muslim, Üsküdar contains neither Jewish residents nor sites of Jewish interest apart from the **cemetery** on the hill just to the left of Bülbüldere Street (between Üsküdar and Bağlarbaşı). Erected in the early 20th century, this cemetery serves the **Sabbatians** (Dönme) who had fled Saloniki. Selanikliler is the name of the road which encircles the cemetery; a reminder of the way the local residents have dubbed these former residents of Saloniki. Members of the sect maintain a small mosque on the cemetery grounds. The Teşvikiye mosque is the starting point for most of the sect's funerals.

This well-preserved cemetery is carefully allocated amongst the various denominations buried within. One plot is designated for people of mixed Sabbatian-Muslim parentage; another for adherents of the Muslim-Shi'ite sect of Istanbul ('Alawis). The third plot — the largest and most impressive — serves two of the three Sabbatian groups of Istanbul: the Kapancılar and Yakubiler. The third group,

Karakaşlar, bury their dead elsewhere.

Amongst the prominent personages buried in this cemetery one will find the grave of the Sabbatian **Şemsi Paşa,** whose tombstone identifies him as "Atatürk'ün Hocası", the teacher of Kemal Atatürk, the founder of the Turkish Republic, back in Saloniki.

Haydarpaşa-Kadıköy

Continuing in a southerly direction, one comes upon the neighborhood of Haydarpaşa, accessible in a variety of ways; (1) by boat from Karaköy to the Haydarpaşa boat station; or from Eminönü and Beşiktaş to Kadiköy; (2) by car, bus or dolmuş via the Üsküdar Terminal; and from the European side over the Bosphorus Bridge to Kadiköy; (3) from Göztepe by train.

The famous **train station of Haydarpaşa** is one of the oldest of the region. Built in the early 20th century, it connected Istanbul to the Holy Cities of Mecca and Medina in the farthest reaches of the Ottoman Empire. This railway played a major role in contemporary Middle East history. Assigned a crucial role in the envisioned Pan-Islam movement of the soon-deposed **Sultan Abdülhamid II,** commandeered by the revolutionary troops of the Young Turks, blown up by the legendary **Lawrence of Arabia** and his Arab Legion, this was also the railroad that established the Israeli Rail System. A plaque was erected in the Ottoman Province of Haifa commemorating the grand occasion of Palestine's first train, which originated here in the train station of Haydarpaşa. Nowadays this station is the starting point for all trains crossing Anatolia, with connecting lines to Ankara and Izmir.

Few Jews resided in Haydarpaşa prior to the late 19th century when a fire which devastated much of nearby Kuzguncuk brought in many Jewish residents. As devout and religious as any of their Jewish brethren in Istanbul, these new settlers wished to build a neighborhood synagogue. Their routine application for a building permit was just as routinely granted, but local factors then entered the story. Orthodox-Greek residents, suspicious of the growing Jewish population, did not stop short of violence in an attempt to halt construction of the synagogue. When the Jews requested the intervention of Sultan Abdülhamid II, who was kindly disposed towards his Jewish subjects, troops were dispatched to restore order, and aid in the construction. The very name of this synagogue, **"Hemdat Israel"** (Hebrew for "The Loveliness of Israel"), echoes the name of the Ottoman sultan Abdülhamid, a discreet compliment to the reigning monarch. The foundation date 5659 (1899) is inscribed on the synagogue gate; the inauguration ceremony was honored by many dignitaries, including the American ambassador **Oscar Straus**.

The large and well-appointed synagogue has been scrupulously preserved. Though not many people attend daily services, the Sabbath and holiday prayers attract a number of Jewish families from the nearby neighborhood of Moda. The synagogue is located at 63, İzzetin Sokak, and can also be reached by Uzun Hafız Sokak which runs parallel. The small connecting alley is graced by a gate bearing the Hebrew inscription "The Holy Congregation of Haydarpaşa and Kadiköy".

Many of the once-Jewish homes surrounding the synagogue are similar to the ones left behind in Kuzguncuk by the new settlers. They, too, bear characteristic Jewish symbols such as *mezuzas* and Stars of David.

A school formed by the Alliance Israélite Universelle system in the late 19th century near the synagogue served the local congregation for nearly 50 years.

The tiny, well-preserved **Jewish cemetery of Haydarpaşa** is located not far away at 13 Zeamet Sokak near Acıbadem Lisesi (tel: 3250692).

The neighboring area of Kadiköy, though lacking sites of Jewish interest, is one of the most attractive of Istanbul, abounding with a profusion of bookstores, galleries, bazaars, old mosques and churches.

Göztepe

This most modern of neighborhoods (including Erenköy-Bostanci-Suadiye) was formerly a summer resort area for many Jews, until the auspious construction of the Bosphorus bridges in 1973 and 1988 rendered the area more accessible for year-round living. Many of the residents make the daily drive into European Istanbul to attend to their businesses.

Some 40% of all Istanbul Jewry currently resides in Göztepe, second in size only to the neighborhood of Şişli. The **Göztepe synagogue**, founded two decades ago, is the religious and cultural center of Jewish life (12, Taş Mektep Sokak, Göztepe; tel: 356 5922; not far from Bagdad Caddesi).

Adjacent to the well-secured synagogue is the modern **Göztepe Jewish Club** (Kültür Derneği; 5, Kemal Salih Sel Sokak; tel: 3504192). Cultural and theatrical activities are conducted regularly for the benefit of the congregation; the magazine *Göztepe Kültür Dergisi* is published on the premises. The two clubs of Göztepe and Şişli together constitute the hub and focus of contemporary Jewish life in Istanbul.

The Princes' Islands (Adalar)

Summer finds a substantial part of Istanbul Jewry in their vacation homes on the Princes' Islands. Most such homes are located on Büyük Ada (The Big Island), but others reside in the Burgaz and Heybeli Islands; Jewish clubs and synagogues are available on all three. Since many of the inhabitants spend only a part of the week in their Island homes, the Jewish community services and prayers are conducted at a somewhat random pace.

Büyük Ada is considered the most prestigious of these islands. The local synagogue, **Hesed Leavraham**, was founded in the middle of this century and is beautifully appointed and well-maintained. Open only during the summer months, the synagogue is located at 5, Pancur Sokak (tel: 3825788).

The synagogue of Burgaz Ada: 2, Köy Kahyası Sokak.

The synagogue of Heybeli Ada: 12/1, Orhan Sokak.

Other Jewish residents prefer not to vacation on these crowded islands, and instead opt for the bright coastal towns of Yalova and Çınarcık on the Asian shore of the Marmara Sea, some two hours away from Istanbul by boat. Others prefer the lovely shores of southern Turkey, especially Bodrum. In neither of these places are there any synagogues.

LIST OF MAPS

FURTHER READING

Akurgal Ekrem, *Ancient Civilizations and Ruins of Turkey*, Ankara: 1983

Anyos Munchos i Buenos. Turkey's Sephardim: 1492-1992, Text by Ayşe Gürsan-Salzmann, photographs by Laurence Salzmann, Philadelphia: 1992

Batman Steven, *The Jews of Byzantium, 1204-1453*, Alabama: 1985

Baudin Pierre, *Les Juifs de Constantinople*, Istanbul ISIS 1989

Benbassa Esther, *Un Grand Rabbin Sépharade en Politique — Haim Nahum (1892-1923)*, Paris: 1989

Braude Benjamin & Bernard Lewis (eds.), *Christians (id Jews in the Ottoman Empire; The unctioning of A Plural Society*, New York: 982.

.ı Hayim, *The Jews of the Middle East, 1860-1972*, New York: 1984.

Çelil. Zeynep, *The Remaking of Istanbul, Portrait of an Ottoman City in the Nineteenth Century*, Seattle: 1986

Elazar Daniel, ed., *The Balkan Jewish Communities*, New York: 1973

Galante Abraham, *Histoire des Juifs de Turquie*, Istanbul: ISIS, 1986, 9 vols.

Gold David, "A Jewish Wedding In Istanbul, January 1981", in *Jewish Language Review*, Haifa, vol. III (1983), pp. 5-10.

Harrel Betsy, *Mini Tours Near Istanbul*, Istanbul: Vol. I-1975, Vol. II-1978.

Karpat H. Kemal, *Ottoman Population 1830-1914, Demographic and Social Characteristics*, Madison: 1985

Lewis Bernard, *The Jews of Islam*, Princeton: 1984

Lewis Bernard, *Istanbul and the Civilization of the Ottoman Empire*, Norman: 1963

Mann B. Vivian, *The Tale Of Two Cities; Jewish Life in Frankfurt and Istanbul 1750-1870*, New York: The Jewih Museum of New York, 1982.

Rodrigue Aaron, *French Jews, Turkish Jews: the Alliance Israélite Universelle and the Politics of*

Jewish Schoolling in Turkey 1860-1927, Bloomington: 1990.

Roth Cecil, *The House of Nasi, The Duke of Naxos.* Philadelphia: 1984

Shalom Gershom, *Sabbatai Sevi, The Mystical Messiah, 1626-1676,* Princeton: 1973

Shaw Stanford & Ezel Kural, *History of the Ottoman Empire and modern Turkey,* 2 vols. London: 1973, 1976.

Shmuelevitz Aryeh, *The Jews of the Ottoman Empire in the Late Fifteenth and the Sixteenth Centuries,* Leiden: 1984

Varol Marie-Christine, *Balat faubourg juif d'Istanbul,* Istanbul ISIS: 1989

Weiker F. Walter, *The Unseen Israelis ; The Jews from Turkey in Israel,* New York: 1988.

Photo Credits:
L. Salzmann pp. 15, 19, 27, 31, 35, 47, 52, 67, 84.

Marie-Christine VAROL

BALAT

FAUBOURG JUIF D'ISTANBUL

LES ÉDITIONS ISIS
ISTANBUL
Şemsibey sok 10
Beylerbeyi
321 38 51

AVRAM GALANTE

HISTOIRE DES

JUIFS DE TURQUIE

9 volumes

LES ÉDITIONS ISIS
ISTANBUL
Şemsibey sok 10
Beylerbeyi
321 38 51